AI in Education Systems: Successful Cases and Perspectives

AI in Education Systems: Successful Cases and Perspectives

Editors

Vadym I. Slyusar

Central Research Institute of Armaments and Military Equipment of Armed Forces of Ukraine, Ukraine; Institute of Artificial Intelligence Problems of Ministry of Education and Science and National Academy of Sciences of Ukraine, Ukraine

Yuriy P. Kondratenko

Petro Mohyla Black Sea National University; Institute of Artificial Intelligence Problems of Ministry of Education and Science and National Academy of Sciences of Ukraine, Ukraine

River Publishers

Routledge
Taylor & Francis Group
NEW YORK AND LONDON

Published 2026 by River Publishers
River Publishers
Broagervej 10, 9260 Gistrup, Denmark
www.riverpublishers.com

Distributed exclusively by Routledge
605 Third Avenue, New York, NY 10158, USA
4 Park Square, Milton Park, Abingdon, Oxon OX14 4RN

AI in Education Systems: Successful Cases and Perspectives / by Vadym I. Slyusar, Yuriy P. Kondratenko.

Routledge is an imprint of the Taylor & Francis Group, an informa business

ISBN 978-87-4380-924-1 (paperback)
ISBN 978-87-4380-926-5 (online)
ISBN 978-87-4380-925-8 (master ebook)
ISBN 978-87-4380-928-9 (ePub)
DOI: 10.1201/9788743809258

Contents

Preface **ix**

List of Figures **xiii**

List of Tables **xv**

List of Contributors **xvii**

List of Abbreviations **xix**

1 General Characteristics of the Large Language Models and Comparative Analysis **1**
V. I. Slyusar, Z. Gomolka, and Y. P. Kondratenko
1.1 Introduction 2
1.2 The Phenomenon of Large Language Models (LLM) and a Brief History 3
1.2.1 The initial stage in the history of LLMs 3
1.2.2 The transformer era 5
1.2.3 Multimodal LLMs 7
1.2.4 Historical overview of the LLM models Gemini, Claude, and Grok 9
1.2.5 Open sources LLMs 12
1.3 Conclusion 14

2 Analysis of Successful AI Applications in the Education Environment **21**
Y. P. Kondratenko, M. B. Solesvik, N. Y. Kondratenko, and Z. Gomolka
2.1 Introduction 21
2.2 Digital and AI Technologies in the Education System 22

2.3 The University Collaboration in AI and IT Fields 27
2.4 Collaboration Between Leading AI Companies and Educational Institutions 31
2.4.1 Potentialities of AI companies for improving educational processes 31
2.4.2 Energetic challenges in the AI field 32
2.4.3 Competition in multi-functional, energy-saving, and low-cost AI tools 33
2.4.4 Successful cases of university-industry collaboration 36
2.5 Conclusion 39

3 AI and Digital Evolution in the Education System of Ukraine **47**
Y.P. Kondratenko, Y.D. Zhukov, A.I. Shevchenko, O.Y. Zhukova, and O.S. Striuk
3.1 Introduction 48
3.2 Digital Evolution and AI Implementation in the Education . 48
3.3 AI's Role in Innovating Shipbuilding Education 57
3.3.1 Drivers and challenges of Ukrainian ship engineering education 57
3.3.2 International academia-business collaboration in navigating Shipbuilding 4.0 59
3.3.3 Discussion of AI tools application and future development 62
3.4 Conclusion 65

4 Best Strategies for Bilingual Education: How Can We Explain Their Success? **75**
Claudia Cabrera, Olga Kosheleva, Christian Servin, and Vladik Kreinovich
4.1 Introduction 75
4.2 Why 50/50 Distribution Between Languages 77
4.3 Why Daily Switches Between Languages 80
4.4 Why It Is Important Not to Correct Minor Mistakes All the Time 81
4.5 Why It Is Important To Regularly Show, To Students, Their Progress 83
4.6 Why It Is Important To Grade Students You Know 83

5 Challenges and Risks of Uncontrolled AI Use by Students and Schoolchildren **87**
Y. P. Kondratenko, N. Y. Kondratenko, and V. I. Slyusar
5.1 Introduction 88
5.2 Peculiarities of AI Use in Learning 89
5.3 Challenges and Risks of Students' Uncontrolled Access . . . 91
5.4 Analysis of the Risks and Special Cases of Uncontrolled AI . 97
5.5 Prospect Ideas for Creating AI 99
5.6 Conclusion 104

6 From Machine Learning to Human Learning: What Can Pedagogy Learn from AI Successes **113**
Victor Timchenko, Yuriy Kondratenko Olga Kosheleva, and Vladik Kreinovich
6.1 Machine Learning and Human Learning – Past, Present, and Future: A Brief Introduction 113
6.2 Who Can Learn? 115
6.3 In What Order Should We Teach? 117
6.4 Related Question: Do We Need Rigorous Foundations? . . . 118
6.5 How Should We Teach: Special Learning Techniques Can Be Helpful, but Is It Possible to Learn Without Them? 119
6.6 How Do We Teach: Is There a Need to Drill on Many Examples? 119
6.7 Need to Balance Positive and Negative Examples 120
6.8 Possibility of Visualization 120
6.9 How to Assess Learning and How to Motivate Students? . . 121

7 Perspectives of AI Applications for Improving Learning and Teaching Processes **125**
V. I. Slyusar
7.1 Introduction 126
7.2 Ecosystem of neuro-coworkers in educational institutions . . 127
7.3 Synthesis of 3D Worlds as an Educational Technology . . . 134
7.4 Large Language Models as a Tool for Acquiring Superknowledge 141
7.4.1 Superknowledge as a new objective of the educational process in higher education institutions 141
7.4.2 Examples of Superknowledge Acquisition through Artificial Intelligence 143

7.4.3 Interaction between Human Knowledge and AI in the Context of Educational Transformation 145
7.4.4 The Era of AGI and Superintelligence 148
7.4.5 A New Paradigm of Education in the Era of AGI . . 153
7.5 Conclusion 158

Index **163**

About the Editors **165**

Preface

This River Publishers Rapid book "AI in Education System: Successful Cases and Perspectives" analyses the current state of art and perspectives artificial intelligence (AI) implementation in education sphere focusing on the successful cases and international experiences as well as on the challenges and risks of uncontrolled AI using by students and schoolchildren.

The book consists of seven chapters and provides an overview of the recent developments in AI tools and successful examples of their practical implementation in teaching and learning processes.

The monograph consists of research-analytic-oriented chapters presented by invited high-caliber scientists from different countries (Norway, Poland, Ukraine and the United States of America).

The chapter "*General Characteristics of the Large Language Models and Comparative Analysis*", by V. I. Slyusar, Z. Gomolka and Y. P. Kondratenko, presents the historical aspects of the of large language models (LLMs) development in the context of their impact on educational processes. Special attention is given to transformer-based models, starting with the emergence of GPT-1 in 2018, Google's BERT, and their subsequent evolution into models such as GPT-4.5, Claude 3.7, and Gemini 2.0. Particular focus is placed on architectural innovations such as the Mixture of Experts (MoE), which enhance model efficiency, as well as the development of open models, including Meta's LLaMa and Chinese LLMs that have become competitive with Western technologies. Recent trends in text generation are also discussed, especially the concept of the Large Concept Model and the new dLLM architecture, which enables faster generation and refinement of textual data. Analyzing the current state of LLMs development, it is noted that these models are already fundamentally transforming education, and their continued improvement opens up new possibilities for integration into the educational domain. The conclusion emphasizes the importance of responsible use of LLMs and the need to strike a balance between their efficiency and the potential challenges they may pose.

In "*Analysis of Successful AI Applications in the Education Environment*", Y.P. Kondratenko, M.B. Solesvik, N.Y. Kondratenko and Z. Gomolka note that AI methods and tools create new opportunities to enhance the efficiency of education systems worldwide. This chapter analyzes successful cases of AI implementation and digital transformation in education, focusing on potential applications in learning, teaching, research, and management. Special attention is given to: (a) successful international experience; (b) inter-university cooperation for AI implementation; (c) collaboration between leading AI companies/consortia and educational institutions; and (d) the role of competition in facilitating AI product integration into education.

Y.P. Kondratenko, Y.D. Zhukov, A.I. Shevchenko, O.Y. Zhukova and O.S. Striuk, in the chapter "*AI and Digital Evolution in the Education System of Ukraine,*" discuss the current state of digital transformation and AI introduced in the Ukrainian education system. Among the focuses are STEM education, SMART technologies, online education and the experience of the leading Ukrainian universities in creating neural networks' ML-laboratory, "Internet of Things" specialization, research laboratory of mechatronics and robotics, innovation ecosystem Sikorsky Challenge, and others. Special attention is paid to (a) innovating shipbuilding education in Ukraine; (b) the development of international academia-business collaboration in navigating shipbuilding 4.0; and (c) analysis of the successful cases and perspectives of AI application in the Ukrainian education system as well as (d) peculiarities of its post-war recovery.

The chapter "*Best Strategies for Bilingual Education: How Can We Explain Their Success?*" by Claudia Cabrera, Olga Kosheleva, Christian Servin and Vladik Kreinovich, discusses that when designing AI-based tools for education, it is important to take into account the experience of teachers. In this, it is necessary to distinguish between the education features that are justified by the general features of the corresponding education task – these features should be taken into account in AI-based learning as well – and features that are specific only to traditional non-AI teaching. In this chapter, on the important example of bilingual education, the authors show that several empirically successful teaching strategies can be explained in the general context and thus should be implemented in AI-based teaching as well.

In "*Challenges and Risks of Uncontrolled AI Use by Students and Schoolchildren*", Yuriy Kondratenko, Nina Kondratenko and Vadym Slyusar analyse the advantages and challenges of artificial intelligence implementation in the education system. The perspectives, potential risks, and dangers of AI use for pupils and students in learning processes and social activities are discussed with illustrations of real cases. Special attention is paid to the proposals and recommendations for the successful integration of AI tools, in particular, large language models, to education processes focusing on the adapted tasks, relevant changing university curricula, increasing critical thinking, ethical challenges, and decreasing risks and dangers of uncontrolled use of AI tools by university students and school pupils. The interaction between AI, artificial conscience, and artificial consciousness within the educational process is discussed.

The chapter "*From Machine Learning to Human Learning: What Can Pedagogy Learn from AI Successes*", by Victor Timchenko, Yuriy Kondratenko, Olga Kosheleva and Vladik Kreinovich, discusses that at this moment, so much experience has been accumulated in AI-based machine learning that it is time to start the analysis in the opposite direction – to see what human-based pedagogy can learn from AI successes. In this chapter, the authors provide the first results of such an analysis.

V. I. Slyusar in the chapter "*Perspectives of AI Applications for Improving Learning and Teaching Processes*" presents the concept of an ecosystem of neuro-coworkers within an educational institution as an innovative approach to integrating large language models (LLMs) into the processes of learning, teaching, and administrative management. The prospects of establishing inter-university networks that facilitate knowledge exchange among educational institutions through a centralized system of federated model training are examined. The use of 3D world generation technologies is discussed as a means for visualizing educational material and applying knowledge in practice, particularly in literature, physics, and mathematics. Special attention is given to the role of artificial general intelligence (AGI) in the formation of superknowledge and the transformation of the educational process at the level of researcher training, with a forecasted paradigm shift in the interaction between human intelligence and AI.

The chapters of the monograph have been structured to provide an easy-to-follow introduction to the topics that are addressed, including the most relevant references, so that anyone interested in this field can get started in the area.

This book may be useful for researchers, policymakers, professors and students who are interested in implementation of advanced AI tools to education system.

Let us express our deep appreciation to all authors for their contributions as well as to reviewers for their timely and interesting comments and suggestions. We certainly look forward to working with all contributors again shortly.

Editors:

Vadym I. Slyusar, Prof., Dr.Sc., Honored Scientist and Technologist of Ukraine, Institute of Artificial Intelligence Problems of the Ministry of Education and Science (MES) and National Academy of Sciences (NAS) of Ukraine

Yuriy P. Kondratenko, Prof., Dr.Sc., Corresponding Academician of the Royal European Academy of Doctors – Barcelona 1914, Corresponding Academician of the RACEF (Spain), Honor Inventor of Ukraine, Petro Mohyla Black Sea National University, Ukraine and the Institute of Artificial Intelligence Problems of MES and NAS of Ukraine

List of Figures

Figure 2.1	Testing results for different LLMs on benchmarks AIME 2024, Codeforces, GPQA Diamond, MATH 500, MMLU, and SWE-bench.	34
Figure 2.2	Directly comparing the performance of the different LLMs.	35
Figure 3.1	Implementation of IS in the education environment.	49
Figure 3.2	Implementation of the laboratory workshop (a) and certificates conferment to graduates of the international group (b).	60
Figure 3.3	Ship Engineering 4.0 supply chain based on the KSERU model.	62
Figure 3.4	Example screen of AVEVA Marine P&ID Integrator Compare Tool (visuals legend: *green* – no inconsistencies, *yellow* – warning, *red* – error, *blue* – unresolved).	63
Figure 3.5	Scheme of the ECCE (executed, checked, corrected, evaluated) AI module.	64
Figure 5.1	Interaction between AI with subsystems and the educational environment.	100
Figure 5.2	New diagram of the interaction between artificial conscience and artificial consciousness within the educational process.	102
Figure 7.1	Teacher's interaction with different student groups during the practical part of the 3D world generation lesson (Ideogram Image Generator).	136
Figure 7.2	A version of the scene from Cinderella, generated using DALLE-3.	139
Figure 7.3	Current phase of the relationship between human knowledge and AI.	146
Figure 7.4	Human consciousness as an unknown object to AGI.	149
Figure 7.5	Mastery of Human Knowledge by SI	151

List of Tables

Table 2.1 Comparison results for Qwen2.5-Max, DeepSeek V3, and Llama-3.1-405B 36

Table 3.1 Selected publications by students as co-authors (Scopus) 55

Table 3.2 AYDU engineers' competencies and educational emphasis 61

Table 3.3 Key Features of the AVEVA Marine P&ID Integrator Compare Tool 64

List of Contributors

Cabrera, Claudia, *Department of Teacher Education, University of Texas at El Paso, USA*

Gomolka, Z., *Department of Computer Engineering, University of Rzeszow, Poland*

Kondratenko, N. Y., *Darla Moore School of Business, University of South Carolina, USA*

Kondratenko, Y. P., *Petro Mohyla Black Sea National University, Ukraine; Institute of Artificial Intelligence Problems, Ukraine*

Kosheleva, Olga, *Department of Teacher Education, University of Texas at El Paso, USA*

Kreinovich, Vladik, *Department of Computer Science, University of Texas at El Paso, USA*

Servin, Christian, *Information Technology Systems Department, El Paso Community College (EPCC), USA*

Shevchenko, A. I., *Institute of Artificial Intelligence Problems, Ukraine*

Slyusar, V. I., *Institute of Artificial Intelligence Problems, Ukraine*

Solesvik, M. B., *Western Norway University of Applied Sciences, Norway*

Striuk, O. S., *Petro Mohyla Black Sea National University, Ukraine; University of Ostrava, Czech Republic*

Timchenko, Victor, *Admiral Makarov National University of Shipbuilding, Ukraine*

Zhukov, Y. D., *National University of Shipbuilding, Ukraine; C-Job Nikolayev, Ukraine; AMICO, Ukraine*

Zhukova, O. Y., *National University of Shipbuilding, Ukraine; MDEM, Ukraine; AMICO, Ukraine*

List of Abbreviations

AI	Artificial intelligence
AI-PPP	AI-powered presentation platform
AMICO	Advanced Measuring Instruments Company
AR	Augmented reality
AYDU	Aker Yards Design Ukraine
BERT	Bidirectional encoder representations from transformers
BSNU	Petro Mohyla Black Sea National University
CC	Concord Consortium
CNN	Convolutional neural network
CSET	Center for Security and Emerging Technology
CSU	Cleveland State University
E2E	End-to-end
ECCE	Executed, checked, corrected, evaluated
EMIS	Education management information systems
EWUP	East-West University Partnership
FLL	Foreign language learning
GPT	Generative pretrained transformer
INSEA	Institute of Novel Ship Engineering Apprenticeship
IR	Intelligent robotics
IRUM	Internal reskilling/upskilling model
IS	Information systems
ITS	Intelligent tutoring system
KPI	Key performance indicator
KSERU	Knowledge-skills-expertise-reskilling-upskilling
LCM	Large concept model
LLE	Lifelong education
LLM	Large language model
LSTM	Long short-term memory
MDEM	Marine Design Engineering Mykolaiv

MIT	Massachusetts Institute of Technology
ML	Machine learning
MMLU	Massive multitask language understanding
MMMU	Multimodal massive understanding
MoE	Mixture of experts
MT	Machine translation
NLP	Natural language processing
NMT	Neural machine translation
NORA	Norwegian AI Research Consortium
NUOS	Admiral Makarov National University of Shipbuilding
OPT	Open pre-trained transformer
P&ID	Process and instrumentation diagram
RAG	Retrieval-augmented generation
RLHF	Reinforcement learning from human feedback
RNN	Recurrent neural network
ROE	Return on experience
SDEU	Ship Design & Engineering Ukraine
SDG	Sustainable development goal
SEC	Southeastern Conference
SFT	Supervised fine-tuning
SMR	Small modular reactor
STEM	Science, technology, engineering, and mathematics
SU	Saarland University
T2I	Text-to-image
TVET	Technical and vocational education and training
USC	University of South Carolina
VR	Virtual reality
WWW	World Wide Web

1

General Characteristics of the Large Language Models and Comparative Analysis

V. I. Slyusar[1], Z. Gomolka[2], and Y. P. Kondratenko[1,3]

[1]Institute of Artificial Intelligence Problems, Ukraine
[2]University of Rzeszow, Poland
[3]Petro Mohyla Black Sea National University, Ukraine
E-mail: swadim@ukr.net; y_kondrat2002@yahoo.com; zgomolka@ur.edu.pl

Abstract

The history of the development of large language models (LLMs) is examined in the context of their impact on educational processes. The analysis begins with the origins of automatic translation, initiated in 1947, and the first imple mentations of this idea, including IBM's machine translation experiments in 1954, the creation of the chatbot ELIZA in 1966, and the evolution of neural network architectures that led to modern LLMs. Significant attention is given to transformer-based models, starting with the emergence of GPT-1 in 2018, Google's BERT, and their subsequent evolution into models such as GPT-4.5, Claude 3.7, and Gemini 2.0. The emergence of multimodal LLMs, capable of integrating text, images, and other data types, is described in detail. Particular focus is placed on architectural innovations such as the mixture of experts (MoE), which enhance model efficiency, as well as the development of open models, including Meta's LLaMa and Chinese LLMs that have become competitive with Western technologies. Recent trends in text generation are also discussed, especially the concept of the large concept model (LCM) and the new dLLM architecture, which enables faster generation and refinement of textual data. Analyzing the current state of

DOI: 10.1201/9788743809258-1

LLM development, it is noted that these models are already fundamentally transforming education, and their continued improvement opens up new possibilities for integration into the educational domain. The conclusion emphasizes the importance of responsible use of LLMs and the need to strike a balance between their efficiency and the potential challenges they may pose.

Keywords: Large language model, LLM, AI, GPT, BERT, LLaMa, large concept model, LCM.

1.1 Introduction

In scientific literature, increasing attention is being devoted to the development of artificial intelligence (AI) technologies in the context of transforming educational processes. One of the most promising directions in this field is the application of LLMs. These neural network-based models are trained on vast volumes of textual data, enabling them to effectively process natural language and address a wide range of text-related tasks. To better understand the LLM phenomenon, it is useful to briefly delve into the history of their development. Naturally, there is no need to examine the entire history of computational automation, which spans several millennia and has already been repeatedly covered in numerous publications. The task is simplified thanks to the works [1, 2], which indicate that the history of LLMs can be traced back to March 1947, when Warren Weaver first shared his ideas on using computers for natural language processing in translation tasks. Weaver proposed this possibility in a letter to cyberneticist Norbert Wiener, with whom he was working at the time on a joint book, and also in a conversation with British crystallographer Andrew Booth, who was visiting the United States to study computer developments. Booth proved to be a very attentive interlocutor and, by 1948, had implemented Weaver's ideas in experiments on "mechanical translation" using punch cards in collaboration with Richard Richens [2].

Let us now examine these historical aspects in more detail, following the perspective of works [1, 2] and other publications on similar topics, while supplementing them with new data that will help better understand the essence of LLMs and their capabilities through the lens of educational needs.

1.2 The Phenomenon of Large Language Models (LLM) and a Brief History of Their Development

1.2.1 The initial stage in the history of LLMs

The history of LLMs, initiated by W. Weaver and taken up by A. Booth, quickly gained momentum. In 1949, newspapers reported that Harry Huskey had also considered the possibility of machine translation using the SWAC computer in Los Angeles [1, 2]. In subsequent years, machine translation research began at the University of Washington (Erwin Reifler), the University of California, Los Angeles (Victor Oswald and Stuart Fletcher), the RAND Corporation, and the Massachusetts Institute of Technology (MIT) [1, 2]. In July 1949, in Carlsbad (New Mexico), W. Weaver presented his memorandum titled "Translation" [3], in which he summarized his views on the prospects of automatic text translation. Of course, this was only an initial conceptual description, and Weaver acknowledged the serious limitations of the simplified approach to solving the task of textual translation. The memorandum noted that the problem of ambiguous word interpretation in translation could be addressed by analyzing the immediate context on both sides of the central word in question. This is essentially how modern LLMs now operate – equipped with attention mechanisms and positional encoding of words. In his optimistic conclusions regarding the future of automatic translation, W. Weaver relied on the McCulloch-Pitts theorem (1943) concerning the mathematical modeling of recursive neural structures in the human brain [2]. In a simplified interpretation, the essence of this theorem can be reduced to the assertion that a neural network model with formally defined regenerative loops, implemented via a computer (Turing machine), is capable of deriving any logical conclusion from a finite set of data. Essentially, the McCulloch-Pitts theorem explains the "intelligence" of modern LLMs and refutes the claims of some researchers who argue that LLMs can only generate conclusions directly encountered during their training. W. Weaver, for his part, saw in this theorem the potential for a formal solution to the problem of automatic translation, based on the logical structure of language syntax and the mathematical computability of logical inference. Supporting this was the finding in [3] that neural networks can implement any computable function that can be executed on a Turing machine. This became a turning point in the development of the general theory of artificial neural networks and LLMs.

According to [2], the reaction to W. Weaver's memorandum was mixed. Some authorities outright rejected the very idea of automating translation, holding views similar to those of professional translators today who fundamentally oppose machine translation. Other experts were less sceptical. One of those who picked up on W. Weaver's proposals was E. Reifler [2], who, over the following months, introduced the concepts of pre-editing and post-editing and proposed the use of regularized languages. An important outcome of Weaver's memorandum was the organization of the first-ever conference on machine translation, held in June 1952 [2]. Further conceptual roots of LLMs can be traced to January 1954, when IBM and Georgetown University collaborated on the first machine translation system, which automatically translated 60 Russian sentences into English using a dictionary of 250 words [1]. Although this experiment was rudimentary, it demonstrated the feasibility of computational language processing and spurred governmental investment in machine translation. Another significant milestone in the history of LLM development was the 1966 demonstration by Joseph Weizenbaum from MIT of the first chatbot psychotherapist, ELIZA [4]. It functioned as a virtual conversational partner that mimicked a psychotherapist using a simple technique of rephrasing user inputs and applying template-based questions. This created the illusion that the bot was conducting a meaningful dialogue. Communication with ELIZA did not occur through a screen but via an electric typewriter connected to a remote computer, with the bot's responses printed out. Despite such a limited interface, some users began to feel an emotional connection with ELIZA and engaged in sincere conversations. This experiment was the first to show that human-machine communication could occur in natural language. At the same time, the most important discovery was that people tend to attribute meaning to chatbot messages on their own, assuming that the machine imbues the text with intent. This phenomenon later became known as the "ELIZA effect," which modern chatbots, such as the one described by Shevchenko et al. [4], have significantly amplified.

The subsequent innovations that contributed to the development of modern LLMs were driven by fundamental breakthroughs in neural network architectures during the 1980s–2000s. In particular, recurrent neural networks (RNNs) emerged in 1986 [5], introducing memory mechanisms for processing textual sequences. The limitations of RNNs due to the vanishing gradient problem were partially addressed in 1997, when S. Hochreiter and J. Schmidhuber invented long short-term memory (LSTM) [6], which employed control mechanisms to retain contextual information over long sequences. The 2010s saw a rapid advancement in deep learning capabilities, spurred by improvements in hardware, datasets, and algorithms. Among the critical milestones was the release of the Stanford CoreNLP toolkit in 2010 [7], which standardized tools for named entity recognition. With the launch of Google Brain in 2011 [8], large-scale neural network training became more accessible, and the introduction of Word2Vec (2013) [9] and GloVe (2014) [10] enabled vector-based representations of semantic relationships.

1.2.2 The transformer era

The earliest attempts to create language models based on large text corpora can be found in works [11, 12]. However, the true breakthrough came with the introduction of the transformer architecture, proposed in 2017 [13], which laid the fundamental groundwork for the development of the first LLMs, such as GPT-1 [14] by OpenAI and BERT by Google [15]. It is worth noting that, in fact, the name "GPT" originated thanks to OpenAI's competitors at Google. Radford et al. [14] at OpenAI described the results of training an unnamed language model based on a 12-layer transformer architecture that included only the decoder part and 12 masked self-attention heads. The context window for inference was limited to 512 tokens. Although the number of model parameters was not explicitly stated in [20], calculations show that it amounted to approximately 117 million. The training dataset used was BooksCorpus, with a total volume of 5 GB, comprising over 7000 unique books of various genres with long sequences of continuous text. In [14], the existing concept of "Generative Pretraining" [16] was used, which was applied to transformers for the first time. Interestingly, however, the authors of [14] did not use the abbreviation GPT or its full form, generative pretrained transformers. Only in October 2018 did the preprint [15] on the BERT language model from Google become the first publication in which the term GPT was officially introduced to describe the model created by OpenAI. It remained in use until the release of OpenAI's next model, GPT-2, in 2019. To differentiate the first model from the new version, the term GPT-1 began to be used for the original model.

Returning to the aforementioned BERT model (bidirectional encoder representations from transformers) by Google [15], it should be noted that its release marked a significant milestone. With 340 million parameters, BERT outperformed previous models on 11 NLP tasks. The implemented method of bidirectional processing allowed the model to analyze entire sentences rather than just token sequences. This enabled a more nuanced understanding of linguistic phenomena. Within 18 months, BERT began handling 90% of

English-language queries on Google, demonstrating its scalability in real-world applications. The release of BERT effectively initiated a competition among LLM developers to build more advanced models – an arms race that has become an integral part of AI advancement for the long term.

In response to the release of BERT, OpenAI developed GPT-2 in 2019 [16], which was significantly scaled up compared to GPT-1 and released in four versions: small (117 million parameters, the same size as GPT-1), medium (345 million parameters, comparable to BERT), large (762 million parameters), and extra-large (1.5 B parameters – the most frequently referenced version of GPT-2). In addition to the increase in size, the architecture was improved, and the context window was expanded to 1024 tokens. Layer normalization was introduced at various stages of the model to enhance stability. The model was trained on a dataset of approximately 40 GB, sourced from a wide range of web pages. As a result, GPT-2 demonstrated substantial improvements in language generation quality, coherence, and versatility. Its ability to produce highly realistic text raised the first concerns regarding potential misuse. This initially led OpenAI to withhold the full version of the model from public release. However, the restrictions were later lifted, and GPT-2 gained recognition as a strong statement of OpenAI's ambition to dominate the LLM domain. The term "Large Language Model" (LLM) gained widespread popularity following the release of OpenAI's preprint on its next model, GPT-3 [17], published in 2020. This work described GPT-3 as a language model with 175B parameters and extensively examined its capabilities across various NLP tasks. Although the concept of large language models had existed earlier, it was this publication that catalyzed the widespread adoption of the term "LLM." It came to denote language models trained on vast text corpora, capable of processing, understanding, and generating text. Notably, the dataset used to train GPT-3 reached 4 TB of data – and this was not yet the upper limit.

The appearance of GPT-3 prompted the entry of a new player into the race for the best LLM – Meta AI Research, which released the Open Pre-trained Transformer (OPT-175B) language model in May 2022 [18]. OPT-175B had the same number of parameters as GPT-3, but it was trained on a dataset containing 180 B tokens, which did not prevent it from demonstrating performance comparable to GPT-3. The main result of the OPT-175B release was the publication not only of the model's code and trained weights but also of a complete operations log that documented the difficulties encountered by developers during the training process. The OPT-175B model was released under a non-commercial license and intended for use by researchers. While full access to the 175B model required submitting an application, smaller versions with 125 million to 30B parameters could be downloaded as part of the HuggingFace Transformers library. In general, it should be acknowledged that the release of OPT-175B undermined OpenAI's monopoly and triggered a significant acceleration of work in the LLM field. The transformer deep learning architecture ultimately became the de facto standard for LLMs, and impressive results were achieved based on it. A significant part of the research was focused on models with an autoregressive decoder only, such as GPT-3 and PaLM, which could perform on par with humans in many NLP and natural language understanding (NLU) tasks.

At present, there is a substantial body of scientific literature dedicated to various aspects of LLMs. These studies demonstrate that LLMs can be effectively utilized for tasks such as machine translation, text generation, summarization with follow-up content-aware dialogue in a question-answer format, and many other functions relevant to educational processes. Further improvements in LLMs, particularly after OpenAI provided public access to ChatGPT on November 30, 2022 [19], have helped further unlock their potential and facilitated their integration into society. The initial ChatGPT service was based on the GPT-3.5 LLM with 175B parameters [19] and marked the first practical attempt to fine-tune an LLM using reinforcement learning from human feedback (RLHF). In January 2023, the number of active monthly ChatGPT users exceeded 100 million for the first time. This milestone enabled OpenAI to introduce exclusive access to its model via the ChatGPT Plus subscription ($20/month), representing the first major attempt at large-scale commercialization of LLM-based services.

In March 2023, with the transition to GPT-4, OpenAI [20] surpassed the threshold of 1 trillion LLM parameters, introduced paid API access to its models for third-party developers, and integrated a plugin ecosystem. The capability to combine text and image processing in GPT-4 was significantly enhanced in September 2023 with the launch of integrated DALL-E 3 image generation access for ChatGPT Plus subscribers. This milestone firmly established the trend in LLM development toward multimodality and enabled OpenAI to gain a decisive lead over its competitors.

1.2.3 Multimodal LLMs

Multimodal LLMs are language models capable of processing and integrating information from various types of data, such as text, images, audio, and video. This approach enables the development of universal systems that can interact with diverse forms of information and provide more natural and multifaceted user interaction. One of the first multimodal LLMs was VisualBERT [21], which combined the previously mentioned BERT language model with visual data processing. This enabled effective handling of text-image combinations and opened up a range of new tasks, such as visual question answering, image captioning, and retrieving images based on textual queries. VisualBERT laid the foundation for further developments in the field of multimodal models, demonstrating the feasibility of integrating various data types into a single system. It is worth noting that similar capabilities can be found in convolutional neural networks (CNNs). For instance, in [22, 23], it is shown that the same neural networks, initially trained for image classification, can also be used for text classification and segmentation. Furthermore, authors [24] explore neural networks for classifying audio signals that simultaneously utilize spectrogram images and time-domain signal sequences analogous to textual sequences. The basis of this phenomenon lies in the formal invariance of digital data processing in neural networks, regardless of the semantic content embedded in the data.

The further development of the ideas introduced in VisualBERT was realized in 2021 through the multimodal model ViLT [25]. In the same year, OpenAI introduced its first multimodal LLM, CLIP [26]. During its training on a large number of text-image pairs, contrastive learning was used to create a shared embedding space for texts and images, enabling tasks such as image classification via text prompts and illustration retrieval based on descriptions. Another project from OpenAI, DALL-E [27], demonstrated the ability to generate images based on textual descriptions. This marked a significant advancement in the field of generative models capable of combining textual and visual information. Building on this experience, OpenAI quickly transformed GPT-3.5 and its successor GPT-4 into the multimodal service GPT-4v, setting a kind of standard for all competitors in the LLM space.

The emergence of many alternative LLMs led to the realization of the idea of combining them using the mixture of experts (MoE) approach, which was advanced by the developers of the Mistral LLM family in their model Mixtral [28]. According to authors in [29], one of the earliest works promoting this architectural concept is considered to be the one in [30]. In the corresponding expert system structure, the output weight vectors of several experts were managed via a specialized gating mechanism. This approach evolved in the context of LLMs such as Mixtral to enhance efficiency and adaptability to various tasks. The core idea of MoE is to distribute input data among different "expert" models based on their specialization. Each expert is optimized to process a specific type of information. After the task is performed by a selected subset of experts, their outputs are aggregated using a gating mechanism that determines the contribution of each expert to the final model output. The remaining experts remain inactive, thus conserving computational resources.

1.2.4 Historical overview of the LLM models Gemini, Claude, and Grok

After the release of GPT-4, several leading companies introduced alternative LLMs that set new standards in the field of AI. Each of these models has a unique developmental trajectory, architecture, and training approach, but all are aimed at achieving high performance and offering a wide range of capabilities.

LLM Gemini is a family of multimodal LLMs developed by the unified team of Google Research and DeepMind following their merger. The Gemini project succeeded Google's earlier AI efforts (such as the PaLM 2 and LaMDA [31] models) and was first introduced in December 2023, when Google announced the release of Gemini 1.0 in three scale variants: Ultra, Pro, and Nano [32]. In early 2024, an update, Gemini 1.5, was released. The Gemini 1.5 Pro version received enhanced performance and an expanded context window of up to 1 million tokens, becoming publicly available in May 2024. This context size became the largest in the industry, allowing the model to "remember" massive volumes of information when solving tasks. The core of the Gemini model was trained simultaneously on different data types (texts, images, audio, code, and video). This represented a significant departure from previous approaches where separate specialized components were trained for each modality, enabling Gemini to analyze images without relying on external OCR systems. Gemini Ultra was the first LLM to surpass human expert performance on the large-scale MMLU (Massive Multitask Language Understanding) knowledge benchmark, scoring 90.0%, compared to $\sim$89% for human experts. This demonstrated the model's ability for deep understanding across various domains (mathematics, physics, history, law, medicine, etc.) and complex logical reasoning, which is highly beneficial in educational contexts. Additionally, on the MMMU (MultiModal Massive Understanding) benchmark, Gemini Ultra achieved 59.4%, the highest score at that time. The development of this LLM line continued with the release of Gemini 2.0 at the end of 2024. In just a short time, Gemini evolved from a prototype to a second-generation model, establishing itself as a key AI platform within the Google ecosystem. Gemini 2.0 introduced new features such as "Deep Research" mode for in-depth exploration of complex topics and further performance enhancements (this version is twice as fast as 1.5 Pro on many tasks). Overall, Gemini has earned a reputation as one of the most powerful and versatile LLMs, approaching the capabilities of OpenAI models and even surpassing them in some metrics.

The Claude models, developed by the company Anthropic (founded by former OpenAI employees), are distinguished by their focus on safety and ethical AI systems. The first version of Claude was officially launched in March 2023 [33]. At launch, Anthropic introduced two variants: Claude, a fully functional high-performance model, and the lighter Claude Instant, designed for speed and cost-efficiency. These models stood out for their better resistance to harmful or inappropriate prompts and a more "obedient" conversational style compared to their contemporaries. In the following months, Claude quickly evolved into Claude 2, which was released in July 2023. At that point, the context window was increased to 100k tokens (the previous version had a context of around 9k tokens). In October 2023, Anthropic introduced Claude 2.1 with a context window of up to 200k tokens. The next major release Claude 3 was announced in March 2024. Claude 3 was launched as a full suite of models of various sizes and purposes: at the top tier of performance was Claude 3 Opus, the mid-tier model was Claude 3 Sonnet, and the compact, fast model was Claude 3 Haiku. The Claude 3 models gained multimodal capabilities and could interpret photos, charts, diagrams, PDF documents, and more. According to Anthropic, at the time of release, Claude 3 Opus outperformed competing models on most standard academic benchmarks – from MMLU (undergraduate-level knowledge) to GSM8K (basic mathematics) and GPQA (graduate-level logical reasoning). According to Anthropic's assessments, the newer versions of Claude were much less prone to unnecessary refusals to answer (so-called cautious or overguarded rejections). Concerned with the safety and reliability of responses, Anthropic developed a new approach called Constitutional AI for training the model to follow a predefined set of values and guidelines when responding to queries. This essentially became the first practical attempt to implement the concept of artificial conscience [34–36], in which a separate critic model reviewed and corrected the primary model's outputs during training. This method allowed Claude to be more "obedient" without the risk of learning undesirable behavior from human error or bias. In practical terms, this means that when asked about questionable or potentially dangerous topics, Claude tries to follow explicitly defined rules (e.g., not aiding illegal activity, avoiding hate speech), rather than relying on a rigid list of prohibitions. After the launch of the third generation, Anthropic continued to iterate: by fall 2024, Claude 3.5 was released, followed by Claude 3.7 (announced in September 2024).

The youngest among the three LLMs discussed in this subsection is Grok. The company xAI was founded by Elon Musk in 2023 with the ambition of "understanding the true nature of the universe" through AI. Musk, known for his criticism of excessive restrictions in chatbots, aimed to create a model that was both powerful and less censored. The first mentions of Grok appeared at the end of 2023, when xAI launched a limited beta access to Grok 1. Reportedly, the early version of the model was trained on data from the social media platform X (formerly Twitter), giving Grok-1 [37] a certain "internet-savvy" character and awareness of contemporary memes and news. In 2024, the Grok project significantly accelerated: an improved version, Grok 1.5, was released, followed by a variant called Grok-1.5 Vision with image support, as well as a smaller model, Grok-1.5 mini, designed for faster responses. Sequential releases included Grok 2 (with a dedicated Grok-2-Vision mode and an agent system under the codename "Aurora"). The culmination came with the official release of Grok 3 in February 2025. xAI claimed that the early version of Grok 3 outperformed competitors – including OpenAI's models and China's DeepSeek model – in a series of tests on mathematics, science, and programming. Throughout 2024, xAI secured significant investments and built a "Colossus" supercomputer powered by thousands of NVIDIA GPUs to train Grok. The model advanced at a remarkably rapid pace: from an initial prototype of ~33 billion parameters in 2023 to an estimated trillion-parameter scale in Grok 3. It is worth noting that xAI takes a rather secretive approach to technical details – no full technical reports or papers about Grok's architecture or datasets have been published. However, Grok 3's architecture is described as "hybrid" or "live," meaning the model has the ability to learn continuously and adapt without catastrophic forgetting. xAI integrated a so-called Deep Search module into Grok – a built-in search engine that provides the model with access to up-to-date online information while responding to queries. As a result, Grok combines generative capabilities with information retrieval features, aiming to always deliver "fresh" and factual responses. Additionally, a "Big Brain" mode is mentioned, which allocates additional computing resources for particularly difficult questions, allowing the model to "think deeper" before responding. This resembles a dynamic adjustment of reasoning steps or expert allocation during task execution. According to some reports, Grok 3 also applies the

MoE (mixture of experts) approach to scale its performance. Although xAI has not confirmed this officially, independent reviews point to "significant architectural improvements" in Grok 3 related to speed and efficiency, and MoE is considered a likely component. As a result, the model's hardware metrics are impressive: Grok 3 is estimated to contain 2.7 trillion parameters and was trained on a dataset of approximately 12.8 trillion tokens. If these figures are accurate, Grok 3 is one of the largest LLMs to date. Such size may be attributed to the use of MoE architecture. The context window of Grok 3 is reportedly around 128k, which is less than that of Claude or Gemini, but still allows the handling of very long conversations or documents. The Grok 3 presentation emphasized the model's "advanced logical reasoning." This aligns with the trend of adding chain-of-thought reasoning to LLMs, where the AI generates intermediate steps in its reasoning. Likely, as with other models, Grok's final fine-tuning involved human feedback (RLHF) to improve the quality of responses. According to OpenCV and other sources, Grok 3 delivers 20% higher accuracy and 25% faster responses than models like ChatGPT (GPT-4). Importantly, the model also consumes approximately 30% less energy due to architectural optimizations.

Overall, the emergence of Gemini, Claude, and Grok has significantly influenced the development of the AI industry, triggering a new wave of competition and laying the groundwork for future technological trends. While at the beginning of 2023 the LLM market was essentially led by a single company (OpenAI with GPT-4), by 2024–2025 the situation had shifted toward multiple centers of innovation. Now, companies such as Google, OpenAI, Anthropic, xAI, as well as Chinese firms (e.g., Alibaba Cloud with the Qwen models [38] or the startup DeepSeek [39]) are competing for dominance. This competition drives all players to accelerate improvements, ultimately benefiting users and businesses by providing access to more powerful and diverse AI systems.

1.2.5 Open sources LLMs

Similar to proprietary models, the development history of open-source LLMs can also be conventionally divided into several stages, each marked by specific technological breakthroughs, shifts in openness policies, and their impact on public ecosystems. OpenAI's decision not to release the code for GPT-3 led to increased activity within the open-source community. In response to closed models, EleutherAI released GPT-Neo and GPT-J (2021), which became the first open analogues to GPT-3. After the launch of

ChatGPT, many companies and research groups began developing their own alternatives. On February 24, 2023, Meta (formerly Facebook AI Research) introduced the LLaMA (Large Language Model Meta AI) family [40], which included four versions with 7B, 13B, 33B, and 65B parameters. These models were trained on 1.4 trillion tokens from open sources such as websites, GitHub repositories, Wikipedia, and others. The main difference from competitors was optimization: LLaMA used a more efficient transformer architecture, which allowed it to achieve GPT-3-level performance with significantly fewer parameters. Meta made LLaMA available to researchers by request, but on March 3, 2023, the model's weight files were unauthorizedly leaked online via BitTorrent, becoming a pivotal event for open-source LLMs. Taking advantage of this, the community quickly adapted the model for use, creating modifications, including integration with the HuggingFace Transformers library and support for running on local hardware.

After the success of the first version, Meta released LLaMA 2 in July 2023 [41], this time officially with open access. The list of main LLaMA 2 versions was reduced to three sizes: 7B, 13B, and 70B. LLaMA 2 quickly became the foundation for numerous open-source projects, including models such as Mistral, Falcon, Zephyr, and many others. In April 2024, Meta introduced LLaMA 3 with 8B and 70B parameter models, followed in July 2024 by LLaMA 3.1, which included models with 8B, 70B, and 405B parameters. The version timeline was further updated in September 2024 with the release of the first multimodal models, LLaMA 3.2 Vision, in 11B and 90B sizes, as well as small language models (SLMs) for text processing with 1B and 3B parameters. LLaMA 3.3 was introduced on December 6, 2024, in a single 70B size; however, due to architecture and training optimizations, this LLM outperformed LLaMA 3.1 405B in some benchmarks. In recognition of Meta's efforts, it should be noted that its LLaMA models became a significant milestone in the development of open language models, providing developers with access to powerful tools for working with NLP.

At the same time, another sharp shift in the balance of power in the LLM domain occurred at the end of December 2024 due to the emergence of several Chinese LLMs: first DeepSeekV3, then DeepSeek R1, and Qwen 2.5 Max, which seized the initiative and opened new opportunities for research, development, and commercial use of language models. Their appearance significantly challenged the dominance of leading models such as OpenAI's GPT-4o, o1, and o3-mini, accelerating the announcement and deployment of new services and LLM versions, the history of which is only beginning. Notably, this includes the presentation of GPT-4.5 on February 27, 2025

[42], the anticipated release of DeepSeek R2 and other models in spring 2025, and the expected debut of the LLaMA 4 family in April 2025. The further development of LLMs, alongside the improvement of their multimodal capabilities, is increasingly characterized by their transformation into large action models based on MoE configurations that combine various types of content processing and generation experts with so-called action agents. These agents are tasked with functions such as creating class schedules, weekend or vacation plans, and other service-oriented actions, which will be discussed in greater detail in chapter 2.

Another notable trend in LLM evolution is the original approach proposed by Meta researchers [43], known as the large concept model (LCM). The key distinction between LCMs and the previously discussed LLMs lies in replacing the traditional next-token prediction with the generation of conceptual units at the level of whole sentences or even entire text corpora. This approach is more radical than token set generation and enables the LCM to track deep semantic relationships and the overall topology of a text. The authors of [43] emphasize that this shift to conceptual-level prediction lays the groundwork for new capabilities in content generation quality, particularly in tasks requiring abstract reasoning and deep comprehension of contextual interrelations.

On the other hand, a fundamentally different approach compared to traditional language models is represented by the new generation of diffusion-based text generators – dLLM [44]. These models start from a noisy block of text and iteratively refine it over multiple stages. This allows for parallel text generation, significantly increasing processing speed (for instance, the Mercury Coder model demonstrates a 5–10x improvement over known LLMs), while also enhancing the global coherence of the generated output. Iterative refinement enables error correction even after the initial generation phase. The dLLM architecture is fully compatible with existing RAG (Retrieval-augmented generation) scenarios and agent-based systems, opening up possibilities for integration into various AI applications. More detailed forecasts regarding the development of LLMs and their transformation into AGI will be discussed in Chapter 7.

1.3 Conclusion

Due to space constraints in this section, many other important players in the LLM field, who have made and continue to make significant contributions to the development of AI, remain outside the scope of the presented historical overview. On the one hand, it is evident that a detailed account of LLM history deserves a separate publication; on the other hand, the turbulence of LLM evolution quickly introduces corrections and leads to the obsolescence of facts previously regarded as cutting-edge achievements, along with the corresponding conclusions. For this reason, the current overview pays less attention to the present state of LLM development – an omission that will be partially addressed in the following chapters of this book. Nevertheless, the conducted analysis indicates that the existing potential of LLMs is entirely sufficient for their effective application and can bring about radical changes in the field of education and science [45–51]. Based on the evolution described above, it is reasonable to expect that LLMs will become even more powerful, integrated, and useful in the coming years. At the same time, the importance of a responsible approach to their use in education will grow, as will the need to strike a balance – one that developers of Claude have attempted to achieve, and which all participants in the LLM race must now take into account.

References

[1] J. Hutchins, 'From first conception to first demonstration: The nascent years of machine translation, 1947–1954: A chronology', Machine Translation 12, 195–252, 1997.

[2] W. J. Hutchins, 'Warren Weaver Memorandum, July 1949,' MT News International, issue 22, July 5–6, 1999. [Online]. Available: https://open.unive.it/hitrade/books/HutchinsWarren.pdf

[3] W. Weaver, 'Translation,' Repr. in: W.N. Locke, A.D. Booth (eds.) Machine translation of languages: fourteen essays,(Cambridge, Mass.: Technology Press of the MIT, 1955), pp. 15 – 23, 1949.

[4] A.I. Shevchenko, V.G. Panok, A.G. Shevtsov, V.I. Slyusar, R.I. Malyi, T.V. Yeroshenko, M.M. Nazar, 'Development of a Virtual Psychological Assistant with Artificial Intelligence in the Healthcare Sector,' Clinical and Preventive Medicine, 2024 (8), pp. 15 – 27, 2024. DOI:10.1145/365153.365168

[5] D. E. Rumelhart, et al., 'Learning representations by back-propagating errors,' Nature, vol. 323, no. 6088, pp. 533–536, 1986. DOI: 10.1038/323533a0

[6] S. Hochreiter, J. Schmidhuber, 'Long Short-Term Memory,' Neural Computation, vol. 9, no. 8, pp. 1735–1780, 1997. DOI:10.1162/neco.1997.9.8.1735

[7] C. D. Manning, M. Surdeanu, et al., 'The Stanford CoreNLP Natural Language Processing Toolkit,' In: Proceedings of the 52nd Annual Meeting of the Association for Computational Linguistics: System Demonstrations, pp. 55–60, 2014. https://nlp.stanford.edu/pubs/StanfordCoreNlp2014.pdf
[8] J. Markoff, 'How Many Computers to Identify a Cat? 16,000', The New York Times. Jun. 25, 2012.
[9] T. Mikolov, et al., 'Efficient Estimation of Word Representations in Vector Space,' *arXiv,* 2013. [Online]. Available: https://arxiv.org/abs/1301.3781
[10] J. Pennington, R. Socher, C. D. Manning, 'GloVe: Global Vectors for Word Representation,' Proceedings of the 2014 Conference on Empirical Methods in Natural Language Processing (EMNLP), pp. 1532–1543, 2014. [Online]. Available: https://aclanthology.org/D14-1162
[11] Y. Bengio, , R. Ducharme, et al., 'A Neural Probabilistic Language Model,' Journal of Machine Learning Research, 3, pp. 1137-1155, 2003.
[12] G. E. Hinton, S. Osindero, Y.-W. The, 'A Fast Learning Algorithm for Deep Belief Nets,' Neural Computation, 18 (7), 1527–1554, 2006. DOI: 10.1162/neco.2006.18.7.1527
[13] A. Vaswani, et al., 'Attention is all you need,' In: Advances in neural information processing systems, pp. 5998-6008, 2017. DOI:10.48550/arXiv.1706.03762
[14] A. Radford, et al., 'Improving language understanding by generative pre-training,' OpenAI, preprint, June 2018. https://cdn.openai.com/research-covers/language-unsupervised/language_understanding_paper.pdf
[15] J. Devlin, M.-W. Chang, K. Lee, and K. Toutanova, 'BERT: Pre-training of Deep Bidirectional Transformers for Language Understanding,' Google AI Language, *arXiv*, 2018. [Online]. Available: https://arxiv.org/pdf/1810.04805v1
[16] A. Radford, et al., 'Language Models are Unsupervised Multitask Learners,' OpenAI, 2019. [Online]. Available: https://cdn.openai.com/better-language-models/language_models_are_unsupervised_multitask_learners.pdf
[17] T. Brown, B. Mann, et al., 'Language Models are Few-Shot Learners,' *arXiv,* 2020. [Online]. Available: https://arxiv.org/abs/2005.14165
[18] S. Zhang, M. Roller, et al., 'OPT: Open Pre-trained Transformer Language Models,' *arXiv,* May 2022. [Online]. Available: https://arxiv.org/abs/2205.01068

[19] OpenAI, 'Introducing ChatGPT', November 30, 2022. [Online]. Available: https://openai.com/blog/chatgpt/
[20] OpenAI, 'GPT-4 technical report,' *arXiv*, 2023. [Online]. Available: https://archive.org/details/gpt-4-technical-paper
[21] L. H. Li, et al., 'Visual BERT: A Simple and Performant Baseline for Vision and Language,' *arXiv,* 2019. [Online]. Available: https://arxiv.org/abs/1908.03557
[22] V. Slyusar, 'Classification of text as images using neural networks pre-trained on the ImageNet dataset,' Artificial Intelligence, 95 (2), pp. 37 - 47, 2023. DOI:10.15407/jai2023.01.037
[23] V. Slyusar, 'The text segmentation by neural networks of image segmentation,' Artificial Intelligence, 98(1), pp. 46 – 55, 2024. DOI:10.15407/jai2024.01.046
[24] V.I. Slyusar, I.I. Sliusar, 'Leveraging pre-trained neural networks for image classification in audio signal analysis for mobile applications of home automation,' Research Tendencies and Prospect Domains for AI Development and Implementation, River Publishers, pp. 109 – 128, 2024.
[25] W. Kim, B. Son, I. Kim, 'ViLT: Vision-and-Language Transformer Without Convolution or Region Supervision,' *arXiv,* Feb. 2021. [Online]. Available: https://arxiv.org/abs/2102.03334
[26] A. Radford, J. W. Kim, et al., 'Learning Transferable Visual Models From Natural Language Supervision,' *arXiv,* Mar. 2021. https://arxiv.org/abs/2103.00020
[27] A. Ramesh, M. Pavlov, et al., 'Zero-Shot Text-to-Image Generation,' *arXiv,* Feb. 2021. [Online]. Available: https://arxiv.org/abs/2102.12092
[28] 'Mixtral of experts. A high quality Sparse Mixture-of-Experts,' https://mistral.ai/news/mixtral-of-experts/
[29] M. Vakulenko, V. Slyusar, 'Automatic smart subword segmentation for the reverse Ukrainian physical dictionary task', CEUR Workshop Proceedings, 2024, vol. 3723, pp. 59 – 73. https://ceur-ws.org/Vol-3723/paper4.pdf
[30] Z.-H. Zhou, 'Ensemble Methods: Foundations and Algorithms' (Chapman & Hall/CRC Machine Learning & Pattern Recognition), 6 June 2012, p. 94.
[31] R. Thoppilan et al., 'LaMDA: Language Models for Dialog Applications,' *arXiv,* Jan. 2022. [Online]. Available: https://arxiv.org/abs/2201.08239

[32] D. Hassabis et al., ‘Introducing Gemini: Our Largest and Most Capable AI Model,’ Google Blog, Dec. 2023. https://blog.google/technology/ai/google-gemini-ai/
[33] Anthropic, ‘Introducing Claude,’ Anthropic News, Mar. 14, 2023. [Online]. Available: https://www.anthropic.com/news/introducing-claude
[34] Y. Kondratenko, G. Kondratenko, A. Shevchenko, V. Slyusar, Y. Zhukov, M. Vakulenko, ‘Towards Implementing the Strategy of Artificial Intelligence Development: Ukraine Peculiarities’, CEUR Workshop Proceedings, 2023, vol. 3513, pp. 106–117. https://ceur-ws.org/Vol-3513/paper09.pdf
[35] Y. Kondratenko, A. Shevchenko, Y. Zhukov, M. Klymenko, V. Slyusar, G. Kondratenko, O. Striuk, ‘Analysis of the Priorities and Perspectives in Artificial Intelligence Implementation’, 13th International IEEE Conference “Dependable Systems, Services and Technologies” (DESSERT’2023), Greece, Athens, 8 p., October 13-15, 2023. DOI: 10.1109/DESSERT61349.2023.10416432
[36] A. I. Shevchenko, M. S. Klymenko, ‘Developing a Model of Artificial Conscience,’ 15th IEEE International Scientific and Technical Conference on Computer Sciences and Information Technologies, CSIT’2020, 23-26 Sept. 2020, Lviv-Zbarazh, vol. 1, pp. 51–54, 2020. DOI:10.1109/CSIT49958.2020.9321962
[37] ‘Open Release of Grok-1,’ xAI Blog, Mar. 17, 2024. https://x.ai/blog/grok-os
[38] Qwen Team, ‘Qwen2-VL: To See the World More Clearly’, Aug. 2024. [Online]. Available: https://qwenlm.github.io/blog/qwen2-vl/
[39] X. Bi, et al., ‘DeepSeek LLM: Scaling Open-Source Language Models with Longtermism,’ *arXiv*, 2024. [Online]. Available: https://arxiv.org/abs/2401.02954
[40] H. Touvron, T. Lavril, et al., ‘LLaMA: Open and Efficient Foundation Language Models,’ *arXiv*, 2023. [Online]. Available: https://arxiv.org/abs/2302.13971
[41] V. I. Slyusar, Y. P. Kondratenko, A. I. Shevchenko, T. V. Yeroshenko, ‘Some Aspects of Artificial Intelligence Development Strategy for Mobile Technologies’, Journal of Mobile Multimedia, Vol. 20_3, pp. 525–554, 2024. DOI:10.13052/jmm1550-4646.2031
[42] OpenAI, ‘OpenAI GPT-4.5 System Card,’ Feb. 27, 2025. [Online]. Available: https://cdn.openai.com/gpt-4-5-system-card.pdf

[43] LCM team et al., 'Large Concept Models: Language Modeling in a Sentence Representation Space,' *arXiv,* 2024. [Online]. Available: https://arxiv.org/abs/2412.08821

[44] 'Introducing Mercury, the first commercial-scale diffusion large language model,' Inception Labs, Feb. 26, 2025. https://www.inceptionlabs.ai/news

[45] A. Laurent, 'La guerre des intelligences à l'heure de ChatGPT,' Lattes, 2023.

[46] Y. P. Kondratenko, V. I. Slyusar, M. B. Solesvik, N. Y. Kondratenko, Z. Gomolka, 'Interrelation and inter-influence of artificial intelligence and higher education systems', Research Tendencies and Prospect Domains for AI Development and Implementation, River Publishers, pp. 31–58, 2024.

[47] Y. Kondratenko, et al. 'Tendencies and Challenges of Artificial Intelligence Development and Implementation,' in: IDAACS'2023 Proceedings, Vol. 1, 2023, pp. 221-226. DOI:10.1109/IDAACS58523.2023.10348800

[48] Z. Gomolka, E. Dudek-Dyduch, Y.P. Kondratenko, 'From homogeneous network to neural nets with fractional derivative mechanism,' Int. Conference on Artificial Intelligence and Soft Computing, ICAISC-2017, L. Rutkowski, et al. (Eds), Part I, Zakopane, Poland, 11-15 June, 2017, LNAI 10245, Springer, Cham, 2017, pp. 52-63. https://doi.org/10.1007/978-3-319-59063-9_5

[49] Y. Kondratenko, et al., 'Machine Learning Techniques for Increasing Efficiency of the Robot's Sensor and Control Information Processing,' Sensors, 22(3), 1062 2022. DOI:10.3390/s22031062

[50] A.N. Tkachenko, et al., 'Evolutionary adaptation of control processes in robots operating in non-stationary environments,' Mechanism and Machine Theory, Vol. 18, No. 4, pp. 275-278, 1983. DOI:10.1016/0094-114X(8)90118-0

[51] R. Duro, et al., (Eds), 'Advances in intelligent robotics and collaborative automation,' River Publishers, Aalborg, 2015. https://doi.org/10.13052/rp-9788793237049

2

Analysis of Successful AI Applications in the Education Environment

Y. P. Kondratenko[1,2], M. B. Solesvik[3], N. Y. Kondratenko[4], and Z. Gomolka[5]

[1]Petro Mohyla Black Sea National University, Ukraine
[2]Institute of Artificial Intelligence Problems, Ukraine
[3]Western Norway University of Applied Sciences, Norway
[4]Darla Moore School of Business, University of South Carolina, USA
[5]Department of Computer Engineering, University of Rzeszow, Poland
E-mail: y_kondrat2002@yahoo.com; marina.solesvik@hvl.no; nina.kondratenko@grad.moore.sc.edu; zgomolka@ur.edu.pl

Abstract

Artificial intelligence (AI) methods and tools are creating novel opportunities to improve efficiency of education systems worldwide. The chapter analyzes successful cases of AI implementation and digital transformation in education, focusing on potential applications in learning, teaching, research, and management. Special attention is given to: (a) successful international cases; (b) inter-university cooperation for AI implementation; (c) collaboration between leading AI companies/consortia and educational institutions; and (d) the role of competition in facilitating AI product integration into education.

Keywords: Education, artificial intelligence, academic consortia, university-industry collaboration, competition, experience.

2.1 Introduction

The education system plays a crucial role in training qualified graduates who contribute to the development of human society across various fields. The successful implementation of artificial intelligence (AI) in disciplines such as biological sciences, industry, agriculture, medicine, space exploration,

DOI: 10.1201/9788743809258-2

marine, air, and ground transportation, and communication [1–7] underscores the necessity of high-caliber AI professionals and highlights the significant potential of university-business collaboration. The integration of AI in control, management, and decision-support processes offers a promising avenue for enhancing educational efficiency through advanced AI tools such as large language models (LLMs), educational robotics, intelligent consultants, natural language processing (NLP), speech recognition and translation, and eye-tracking technologies [8, 9].

Today, AI tools are increasingly integrated into education systems globally. Analyzing international experiences and successful AI applications in education can enhance their potential in learning, teaching, research, and management. Knowledge exchange is particularly crucial for both developed and developing countries, given the rapid evolution of AI and the global competition (United States, China, European Union, and others) for leadership in this field. When promoting innovative AI technologies in education, it is essential to consider: (a) international best practices in AI-driven educational processes; (b) opportunities for academic collaboration to benefit partner universities; (c) the potential for academic-industry cooperation through shared resources, faculty involvement in AI research projects, and industry professionals contributing to teaching; and (d) the competitive situation among AI companies striving to develop multi-functional, energy-efficient, and cost-effective AI tools that simplify educational integration.

This chapter aims to analyze successful cases of digital and AI technology implementation in education based on international experience, inter-university cooperation, and university-industry (U-I) consortia, while providing practical recommendations for optimizing AI-driven learning and teaching processes.

The rest of the chapter consists of four sections. The successful cases of digital technology and AI applications in education based on international experiences are discussed in Section 2.2. Section 2.3 explores inter-university cooperation for mutual benefits in AI utilization. Section 2.4 examines the collaboration between leading AI companies and educational institutions. Section 2.5 presents the conclusions.

2.2 Digital and AI Technologies in the Education System Based on International Experience: Successful Cases

The digital transformation toward Industry 4.0 necessitates that students develop specialized competencies and skills, anchored in the correlation and interconnection of modern AI methods and tools with advanced and modified learning-teaching methodologies.

Educational institutions worldwide are striving to update and enhance curricula for two primary student categories: (a) computer science students specializing in the AI and information technology (IT) fields; and (b) students from other disciplines who require proficiency in applying AI tools to address real-world challenges in their respective domains (law, medicine, business, social science, architecture, agriculture, etc.). Graduates must be equipped to adapt to roles across various industries, aligning with their educational backgrounds, and to tackle dynamic tasks amidst rapid advancements in AI software and hardware.

Educational strategy for digital transformation. AI technology is a pivotal technical actor in the fast evolution of our educational environment. Supporting a modern workforce is based on the successful incorporation of modern AI technologies into existing education processes. A deficiency in AI-related skills could hinder individuals' competitiveness in the job market.

The international experience of 10 countries (Australia, Germany, Ireland, Estonia, New Zealand, Finland, Portugal, Singapore, Scotland, and Slovenia [10]) reflects the peculiarities of digital technology implementation for the successful modernization of existing teaching and learning processes. Among the discussed directions in digital education strategies are teachers' competencies in digital technologies and their continuing professional development; students' digital literacy and digital maturation; tackling digital inequalities; application of AI for personalizing learning, supporting students with special needs [10, 11], transcribing teachers' spoken language into text and evaluating advanced methods in the digital transformation of educational processes.

The main aspects of AI educational strategy for digital transformation are discussed in a study [12] analyzing the AI tendencies, trends, and challenges for academic institutions, advanced interactive modes in human-computer communication, and intelligent design for graduates who will work in the companies of the future as well as a successful AI-driven educational technology for learning courses, innovation and research projects, internships, internationalization, and entrepreneurship initiatives. Special attention is paid to reconsidering and renewing the university curricula using the educative model Tec21 [12], which structures the courses based on the advantages of mixed teaching methodologies, combination of the virtual and physical laboratory works and perspectives of problem-based learning approaches according to demands of Industry 4.0, with the goal implementing

AI academic programs corresponding to requirements of the twenty-first century.

University's curricula modification. To align university curricula with advancements in AI design and international best practices, it is necessary to develop specific recommendations for the efficient implementation of AI tools and modern digital technologies in learning structures and pedagogy. The education system requires a diverse array of techniques to enhance university graduates' skills and disseminate contemporary AI knowledge throughout their training. Discussions on modifying university curricula for graduate students, based on cutting-edge research in AI, IT, advanced control, and decision-making theories, have been presented in a work [13]. Successful examples from USA and Ukraine institutions, such as the Washkewicz College of Engineering at Cleveland State University (CSU) and Petro Mohyla Black Sea National University, demonstrate the effectiveness of the proposed approaches.

Typically, university curricula comprise mandatory and elective courses, with elective options updated annually to reflect new developments in IT and AI. In particular, the M.Sc. program in Electrical Engineering at CSU [13] includes different groups of elective courses which correspond to specific specializations. Among these courses are: modern digital design, software design and architecture, rapid digital system prototyping, embedded systems, high-performance computer architecture, mobile computing, parallel processing systems, and others. For example [13], (a) 10 elective courses are proposed for students in the Control Systems specialization and (b) 14 elective courses for students in the Computer Systems specialization.

The Internet and World Wide Web (WWW) technology opened promising avenues for incorporating modern AI methods and tools into educational processes. B. Collis and J. Moonen (University of Twente, the Netherlands) described the peculiarities of flexible education in a digital world [14], including flexible learning, the use of computer-based learning, and WWW-based course-support systems in education. Four key components influencing the success of flexible learning include technology, pedagogy, implementation strategies, and institutional frameworks, alongside the technological and financial support of education.

Personalized education and artificial intelligence. Globally, education systems are shifting toward personalized or student-centered approaches to accommodate students' diverse cognitive abilities, aspirations, preferences, and desires for in-depth knowledge across various subjects, as well as varying physical conditions. Efficient educational technology (EdTech) startups, substantial government funding in AI research, and innovations such as Big Data, Machine Learning (ML), and AI can facilitate understanding of individual student needs, paving the way for "personalized trajectories" in education. This "student-centered" approach allows for curriculum modifications based on graduates' qualifications, skill requirements, and individual learning capabilities.

The dynamic progression of AI-driven educational development offers new prospects for personalized education in the near future. Bhutoria [15] studies and analyzes the experience of three countries (India, USA, and China) in developing AI-driven personalized education based on their pioneering experience in EdTech innovations and their great contributions to developing global education systems. The analysis results demonstrate the efficiency of AI in satisfying specific learning requirements, preferences, and abilities of students by orienting them into optimal-personalized learning trajectories. AI can tailor educational content to students' needs and desires, transforming education into a more interactive and motivating system by improving educational content, creating opportunities for sharing teaching, library, and computer resources, introducing such modern technologies as VR (virtual reality) and AR (augmented reality) [16], etc.

India's experience shows that schools [17] are beginning to move from traditional teaching methods to smart education. Personalized learning, adaptive assessments, and recommendation systems are an important result of AI-driven learning platforms, which help students and support teachers. At the same time, such technologies [17] as facial recognition, image processing, emotion recognition, and NLP require more wide adoption by Indian EdTech companies. Integrating such AI tools internationally in the future could substantially enhance the teaching-learning processes.

International students' success and AI. Implementing AI tools in education presents numerous opportunities for international students, whose numbers are projected to reach eight million by 2025. Nevertheless, these students have different difficulties and challenges in studying abroad, prompting universities to investigate AI tools for improving the educational environment. The authors [18] (a) study the AI influence on the comfort and quality of education of international students based on different AI applications, in particular, adaptive testing, personalized learning experiences, predictive analytics, and large language models; (b) discuss cultural and privacy aspects, diversity, foreign language difficulties, ethical challenges, etc. [18]. As an emerging field, AI plays a significant role in supporting international education by balancing the advantages and disadvantages of AI technology and adapting university curricula based on modern AI educational technologies.

UNESCO's role in AI implementation in the education sphere. UNESCO is the United Nations' specialized agency for education, which provides support to national education systems, leadership on regional and global levels, and solves contemporary global challenges in the education sphere. Additionally, UNESCO is entrusted with leading and coordinating the Education 2030 Agenda. UNESCO's working paper "Artificial Intelligence in Education: Challenges and Opportunities for Sustainable Development" [19] highlights that AI is a rapidly advancing technological domain with the potential to transform various aspects of society. AI generates various innovative educational solutions that are successful in different contexts. The working paper [19]: (a) forecasts the level of AI impact on the education system, (b) presents numerous successful examples of AI integration in education worldwide, and (c) discusses multiple AI-driven approaches for the success in sustainable development goal 4 (SDG 4), which aims to ensure inclusive and quality education for all. Furthermore, the working paper [19] identifies key policy implications of AI in education, focusing on four main challenges: (1) ensuring inclusive and equitable introduction of AI in the education environment; (2) applying AI to improve teaching and learning processes; (3) promoting skills development for the changing labor market in the AI era; and (4) providing transparency and accountability of education information.

Among the successful AI implementations in national education systems of various countries are:

(a) AI is used to promote personalized learning and improve educational outcomes (Brazil, China, South Africa, Uruguay, and Kenya).
(b) AI-driven data analytics are enhancing education management information systems – EMIS (Bhutan, Chile, United Arab Emirates, Kenya, and Kyrgyzstan).
(c) AI is shaping new curricula for a digital and AI-powered world (Argentina, European Union, Estonia, United Kingdom, Singapore, and Malaysia).
(d) AI is strengthening educational potentialities through advanced post-secondary education and training programs (France, China, and South Korea).

It is evident that AI offers significant potential for improving education systems globally. However, policymakers must continuously evaluate successful international practices while considering national contexts, challenges, and the risks and dangers associated with AI introduction into the education systems.

2.3 The University Collaboration in AI and IT Fields

Collaboration between universities within academic consortia is an effective way to improve the education quality in the AI and IT fields [20–23]. Globalization and internationalization have significantly encouraged inter-university collaboration, helping institutions enhance their global competitiveness. Individual universities can provide their students with greater opportunities by sharing AI and IT resources with partner institutions. Inter-university cooperation is a well-established academic tradition at both national and international levels, enabling resource sharing for mutual benefit and increased efficiency. Some of the most advanced universities have successfully implemented collaborative initiatives such as WASP-Ed, Horizon Europe, EIT, and Erasmus+ [24].

The successful design of national inter-university collaborations depends on selecting suitable technical educational platforms and optimizing the organization of collaborative processes. Modern universities should take into account: (a) very dynamic changes in new technologies based on the implementation of LLMs (ChatGPT, Llama, Bard, Gemini, Mistral, etc.); (b) the need to introduce new courses for studying modern AI tools; (c) the creation of innovative educational models such as platform universities and colleges; and (d) the growing demand for virtual learning environments that facilitate online teaching and collaborative learning.

Networking is a promising strategy for fostering strategic partnerships between universities and enhancing competitiveness in the international educational market. It enables institutions to achieve outstanding results by combining complementary expertise and resources, accelerating decision-making, enhancing responsiveness to technological innovations, and fostering long-term trust-based relationships. Networking cooperation in higher education helps the coherence of universities' positions in their common education policy [25].

Let us consider some successful cases of inter-university cooperation in the different countries and continents.

Case 1. A successful example of inter-university cooperation is the *Swedish National Initiative* for creating inter-university collaboration for AI implementation in the national education system. The most popular educational platforms in use at Swedish universities are Canvas (Sunet), Lisam, Blackboard/Blackboard Ultra, Its Learning, O365/SharePoint*, Moodle, and others. WASP-Ed is a Swedish initiative for creating a network of universities at the national level for collaboration in the AI field [24]. The WASP-Ed collaboration is based on the partnership of eight universities in AI technology with a perspective for extension to 30+ Swedish universities as partners.

Case 2. Another successful example deals with the Chinese *East-West University Partnership* (EWUP), which connects over 220 institutions across the country [26]. The partnership is based on the strategic improvement of the potential of collaborative universities to facilitate the development of talents, new knowledge, and other resources in China's higher education. EWUP must pay special attention to managing long-term university partnerships between diverse (more and less developed) regions.

Case 3. European University Alliances and Consortia stimulate new approaches in education by introducing innovative components in their project structures. In particular, the *Ulysseus European University Alliance* [27] includes the University of Seville (Spain), Technical University of Košice (Slovakia), Université Côte d'Azur (France), Haaga-Helia University of Applied Sciences (Finland), University of Genova (Italy), University of Münster (Germany), MCI/The Entrepreneurial School (Austria), and University of Montenegro. Ulysseus Consortium focuses in the AI field on (a) Applied AI for business and education and (b) facilitating the implementation of AI into practice. Ulysseus is the center of gravity for partners' collaboration with an emphasis on AI-driven education, increasing research efficiency, and searching for novel methods in knowledge transfer while simultaneously spreading and deepening European values.

Case 4. Virtual learning environments become very popular especially when applied to online teaching and learning. ITC-Euromaster with inter-university collaboration concept [28] helps (a) to improve the knowledge transfer and experience exchange in IT implementation; (b) to increase the efficiency of research in the different subject fields with IT applications; (c) to develop and extend the ITC-Euromaster partner-network and create better conditions for successful collaboration between educational institutions as members of such network. In particular, ITC-Euromaster realizes an advanced M.Sc. program for AEC specialization (architecture, engineering, construction) [28]. The main components of the ITC-Euromaster are (a)

Moodle (virtual learning environment), and (b) Adobe Connect Pro (virtual classroom, where teachers can directly communicate with their students). The universities, which are members of ITC-Euromaster's education network, create a common set of training courses and can elect any desired courses from this set for their students. The virtual learning space is created by uniting and sharing the technical and organizational resources of *five higher education institutions* from Austria (University of Technology Graz), Slovenia (University of Maribor and University of Ljubljana), and Ireland (University College Cork and Dublin Institute of Technology).

Case 5. The European Universities Initiative is an EU program aimed at fostering alliances between European universities. A successful example is ***NEOLAiA***, one of the European university consortia [29]. NEOLAiA is an alliance of eight young European universities from Spain, Germany, the Czech Republic, Sweden, Italy, Lithuania, Romania, France, and Cyprus. It was established as a strategic collaboration initiative in May 2019. The alliance has launched numerous institutional collaboration activities, covering areas such as teaching and learning (with a total grant of €399,670.4), research, inclusion and diversity, mobility, entrepreneurship, and employability.

Case 6. The American *Inter-University Consortium for Doctoral Courses* in RBFM (public budgeting, finance, and financial management) was created in the framework of online doctoral programs. Seven universities are members of the consortium, including the University of Maryland, the University of Colorado-Denver, Georgia State University, Syracuse University, the University of Georgia, the University of Kentucky, and Northern Illinois University. The consortium experience provides valuable insights from its pilot phase and offers opportunities for future improvements. The authors of a study [30] anticipate that this initiative could serve as a successful model for university collaboration in the future.

Case 7. The international *UNITWIN/UNESCO Chairs Program* united 950 chairs at educational institutions from 120 different countries [31], focusing on international collaboration in TVET (technical and vocational education and training). The successful experience of the UNESCO Chair on digitalization in TVET (Shenzhen Polytechnic University, China) is discussed in a study [31], where authors also analyze (a) different approaches to accelerating digital transformation in TVET; (b) conditions for long-term and stable international partnerships; (c) digital disparities in different regions and countries; and (d) generalize digital transformation experience with efficient proposals for increasing quality of TVET.

Other successful cases. The authors in similar studies [8, 32] analyzed successful academic consortia that focus on AI implementation in education, in particular:

- *Norway*: The partnership in *NORA* (*the Norwegian AI Research Consortium*) is based on mutual institutional interests in AI, ML (machine learning), and IR (intelligent robotics). Sixteen establishments are members of NORA, including universities, colleges, and research institutes.
- *United States*: (a) The *Concord Consortium (CC)* is situated in two locations: Concord, Massachusetts and Emeryville, California. Tufts University, McGraw-Hill Education, the New York Hall of Science, the University of Illinois, the National Geographic Society, and other institutions successfully collaborate with the CC consortium. In particular, the CC consortium, together with the University of Florida, Texas Tech University, and WestEd (San Francisco, CA), is creating a one-year certificate program "Artificial Intelligence in Math"; (b) The *SEC (Southeastern Conference) Artificial Intelligence Consortium* has implemented a new course, "Teaching with AI @ Auburn," developed by Auburn University. The SEC AI consortium includes 16 partner universities, namely: University of Alabama, University of Arkansas, Auburn University, University of Florida, University of Georgia, University of Kentucky, Louisiana State University, University of Mississippi, Mississippi State University, University of Missouri, University of Oklahoma, University of South Carolina, University of Tennessee, The University of Texas at Austin, Texas A&M University, and Vanderbilt University.
- *Africa*: The *Artificial Intelligence Africa Consortium* unites universities, research institutions, and government agencies that are interested (Cirrus Program) in the development and application of AI methods and tools in education systems and other sectors of the African economy.
- *Thailand*: One of the main goals of the *Thailand Artificial Intelligence University Consortium* is to create a national AI skills development initiative taking into account the entire AI capabilities of the partner institutions.

Scientists worldwide have devoted significant attention to analyzing the effectiveness of inter-university consortia, facilitating the exchange of best practices, and promoting collaboration among partner universities and the broader educational community. These efforts include sharing innovative AI tools, methods, and research findings through academic publications, books, reports, and conference proceedings [33–35]. Academic consortia and inter-university cooperation in the fields of AI and IT represent a well-established global practice. These initiatives serve as an effective approach to training highly skilled university graduates, who are in high demand in the technology sector and contribute to improving people's quality of life in the future.

2.4 Collaboration Between Leading AI Companies and Educational Institutions

Increasing the training quality of students in AI specialization can also be efficiently achieved by collaboration between universities and AI companies in the framework of University-Industry consortia [7, 8, 21, 36]. AI companies have and control huge computing resources for powering AI systems. Universities, colleges, and schools have not or have only limited access to such resources, which leads to disparities in AI development and application with significant implications for AI safety and societal progress. As members of U-I consortia, AI companies can share computing and other expensive resources with university partners.

Successful international experience in education development illustrates that in many cases, cooperation within U-I consortia can be efficiently based on multi-year activity programs for improving education processes, conducting joint research, data exchange, sharing resources, and so on [8, 37, 38].

2.4.1 Potentialities of AI companies for improving educational processes

LLMs and other AI tools developed by leading AI companies hold significant potential for expanding their application in educational processes. For example, machine translation has advanced substantially over the past few decades, primarily due to neural networks, which were trained using huge datasets. However, in many cases, it is difficult or impossible to find sufficient training data for languages with minor speakers [39]. This limitation has restricted the range of languages that AI translation models can effectively support. Researchers at Meta (Menlo Park, California, USA) [39] have developed a machine-learning system capable of translating the original speech in 101 languages into spoken words in any of 36 target languages. The SEAMLESSM4T (massively multilingual and multimodal machine translation) system can also translate text to text, speech to text, and vice versa. Meta's LLM LLaMA was successfully released for academic research worldwide, and as the next step, Meta has made SEAMLESSM4T available as open-source software.

American companies Scale AI (San Francisco, California) and NVIDIA (Santa Clara, California) have partnered to advance generative AI with NeMo SteerLM [40]. This collaboration enables new opportunities for the education sector by allowing developers to create AI-powered applications adapted to the own requirements and desires of teachers and students.

Leading AI companies also support AI education by organizing lectures, seminars, and webinars. For instance, Amazon has launched the "AI Ready" initiative, committing to providing free AI skills training to two million people by 2025 [40]. This initiative includes eight free AI courses, $12 million in generative AI scholarships, and a partnership with Code.org to promote AI education accessibility.

A. Karpathy, who was in different years a founding member at OpenAI, Sr. Director of AI at Tesla, and in 2024 started a new AI+Education company "Eureka Labs," released one of the best "Intro to LLMs" on YouTube [40]. This lecture covers training, inference, jailbreaks, fine-tuning, the emerging LLM OS, and LLM Security. Company Eureka Labs is building a new kind of AI school [41], where an optimizing AI teaching assistant can help teachers design the course materials on a common platform. Eureka Labs is developing the world's best AI course, LLM101n, for the bachelor's educational level [41].

2.4.2 Energetic challenges in the AI field

Today, most AI companies require huge energy supplies for the efficient functioning of the data centers and computing facilities. Data centers are facing a shortage of electricity as the demand for AI is growing fast [42]. This is causing concerns about the strain on the power grid and competition for resources. To address this issue, data centers with built-in nuclear reactors have begun to be developed. An example is the small modular reactor (SMR). This is a design for an advanced reactor capable of producing about a third of the electricity of a traditional large nuclear plant. An AI-driven data center requires approximately 80 megawatts of electricity, compared to 32 megawatts for a conventional data center – 2.5 times more energy consumption.

Google discussed with Kairos Power (Alameda, California) about supplying nuclear energy using small modular reactors [43]. According to the joint agreement, first SMR must be ready by 2030 and additional SMRs during the next 5 years should potentially provide up to 500 megawatts of carbon-free power.

Similarly, Amazon has agreed to purchase power from X-Energy Reactor Company (Rockville, Maryland). The reactors are planned to be built in Washington State [44] with an investment of 0.5 billion USD from Amazon. These partner activities will be supported by innovating SMR startups to design smaller, cheaper, and safer reactors.

Microsoft plans to purchase power that will be produced by restarting the 835-megawatt reactor in Pennsylvania [44] at the Three Mile Island nuclear plant.

2.4.3 Competition in multi-functional, energy-saving, and low-cost AI tools

China announced in 2017 the country's plan to be an AI leader on the international level by 2030 and tasked the Chinese industry to create disruptive AI tools by 2025 that should be highly competitive on the world stage [1, 4, 45]. According to the report of the CSET (Center for Security and Emerging Technology at Georgetown University, USA), 440 Chinese universities (by 2022) were approved by the government for training students with AI specialization at the bachelor's level. In 2022, China accounted for approximately 50% of the high-caliber AI researchers, compared to 18% in the United States [45].

The National Engineering Laboratory for Deep Learning Technology and Application led by technical company Baidu from Beijing (China), has trained thousands of AI specialists.

To be a leader in the world in AI development and implementation is a goal of policymakers, businessmen, and scientists of many high-tech countries. For example, US President Donald Trump announced a private-sector initiative to transform AI infrastructure in the United States. Named the Stargate Project, this ambitious endeavor involves collaboration between OpenAI, SoftBank, and Oracle [46]. The project aims to scale up to $500 billion within four years. The Stargate initiative is designed to solidify America's leadership in AI development while enhancing economic growth and national security. Executives from OpenAI, SoftBank, and Oracle revealed that the project's first phase will focus on constructing advanced data centers. President Trump also predicts that Stargate will create "over 100,000 American jobs almost immediately."

At the same time, Chinese scientists create a new non-expensive LLM "DeepSeek R1." DeepSeek's advanced approach significantly decreases costs for design and training processes [47] compared with OpenAI, Meta, Google, and Microsoft. DeepSeek is trended on Google and has also become #1 among free apps in the Apple Store in the US, UK, and China [48]. While OpenAI charges $15 per million tokens via its API, DeepSeek offers a much lower cost of $0.55 per million tokens [49]. DeepSeek-R1 models generate responses step-by-step akin to human reasoning [50]. Research from Berkeley [49] suggests that cutting-edge reinforcement learning can be achieved without the substantial budgets of industry giants like OpenAI, Google, and Microsoft. These advancements have also challenged assumptions that AI development will require massive electricity consumption, raising new questions about the future of energy demands in the AI sector [51].

Figure 2.1 presents a comparative analysis [50] of LLM models, including DeepSeek-R1, OpenAI-o1-1217, DeepSeek-R1-32B, and OpenAI-o1-mini.

The 39-year-old company founder Wenfeng Liang, who graduated from Zhejiang University (Hangzhou, China) with a degree in computer science, established DeepSeek in 2023. DeepSeek also developed the Janus-Pro-7B model, which, using text description, can create different images in the same style as DALL-E 3, developed by OpenAI (San Francisco, USA), and Stable Diffusion, developed by Stability AI (London, UK) [45].

However, DeepSeek's success has led to competition among domestic companies to upgrade their own AI models. AI companies MoonshotAI and ByteDance claim that their new models, Kimi 1.5 and 1.5-pro, can outperform GPT-4o1 on some benchmarks [45].

Qwen is a family of LLMs introduced by Chinese technology company Alibaba in September 2023, based on the Llama models released by the

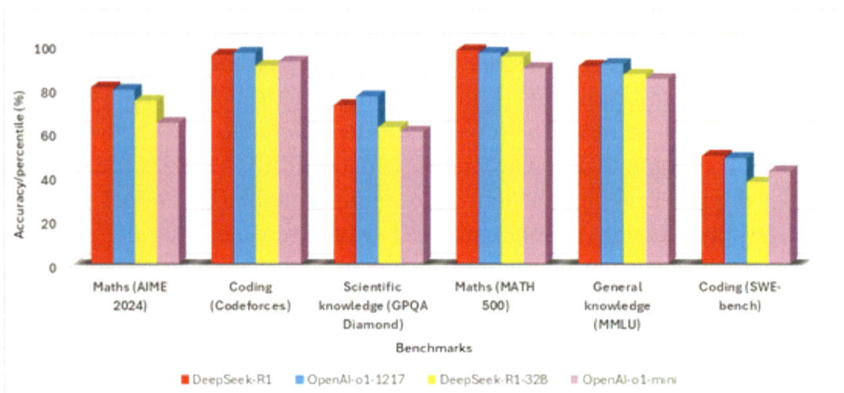

Figure 2.1 Testing results for different LLMs on benchmarks AIME 2024, Codeforces, GPQA Diamond, MATH 500, MMLU, and SWE-bench.

American company Meta. Alibaba released an advanced LLM, Qwen 2.5, and is developing Qwen 2.5-Max [52], a large-scale mixture of expert (MoE) model. Twenty trillion tokens were used for MoE pre-training with post-training based on such methodologies as SFT (supervised fine-tuning) and RLHF (reinforcement learning from human feedback). In its announcement, Alibaba emphasized that Qwen 2.5-Max in many cases outperforms such LLMs as GPT-4o, DeepSeek-V3, and Llama-3.1-405B [53]. Comparative results for the performance of different LLMs [52], including Qwen 2.5-Max, DeepSeek V3, GPT-4o, Llama-3.1-405B, and Claude-3.5-Sonnet, are presented in Figure 2.2.

Qwen 2.5-Max outperforms DeepSeek V3 in benchmarks such as Arena-Hard and GPQA-Diamond and also demonstrates competitive results in other assessments, including MMLU-Pro. Comparison results are also presented in Table 2.1, where Qwen 2.5-Max (Alibaba) was evaluated against DeepSeek V3 (DeepSeek) and Llama-3.1-405B (Meta) [52].

Concurrently, two advanced reasoning models of the Grok 3 series are introduced by Elon Musk's AI startup xAI [54]. Grok 3 was called by Mask as "the smartest AI on Earth," underlining its high ability in reasoning and

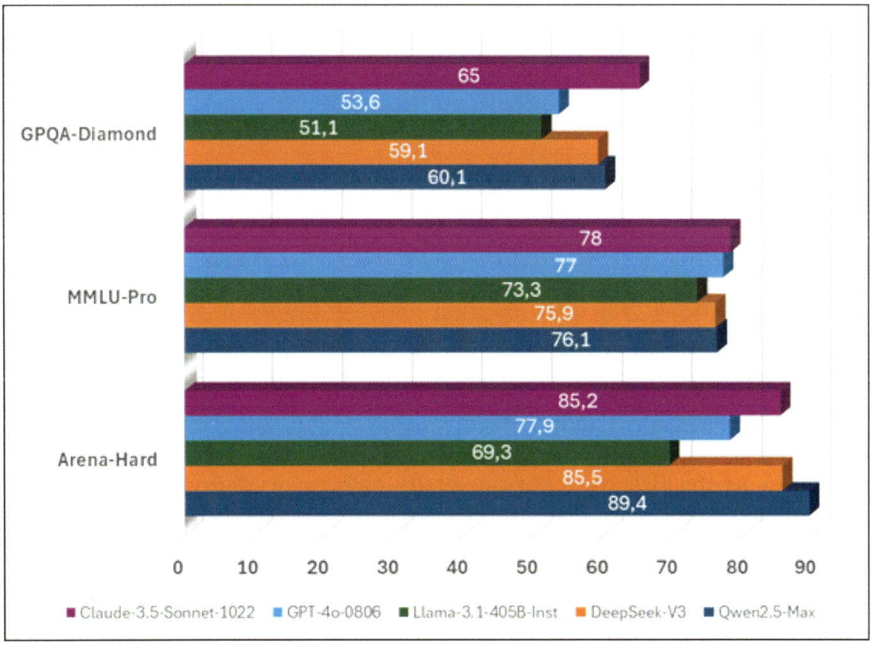

Figure 2.2 Directly comparing the performance of the different LLMs.

Table 2.1 Comparison results for Qwen2.5-Max, DeepSeek V3, and Llama-3.1-405B

No.	Test/LLM	Qwen2.5-Max	DeepSeek-V3	Llama-3.1-405B
1	MMLU	**87.9**	**87.1**	**85.2**
2	BBH	**89.3**	**87.5**	**85.9**
3	C-Eval	**92.2**	**90.1**	**72.5**
4	CMMLU	**91.9**	**88.8**	**73.7**
5	HumanEval	**73.2**	**65.2**	**61.0**
6	MBPP	**80.6**	**75.4**	**73.0**
7	CRUX-I	**70.1**	**67.3**	**58.5**
8	CRUX-O	**79.1**	**69.8**	**59.9**
9	GSM8K	**94.5**	**89.3**	**89.0**
10	MATH	**68.5**	**61.6**	**53.8**

decision-making. xAI's test results show that Grok 3 has very high speed in big data processing, increasing accuracy and decreasing the amount of mistakes and hallucinations.

As the AI field grows increasingly competitive, the ability to adapt quickly becomes a vital asset. Considered examples demonstrate that strong competition for leadership in AI development has some perspectives and advantages for the fast and wide implementation of modern AI tools in the education system. This is because AI systems within design processes on the competition base will become cheaper, less energy-consuming, and more accessible for universities and educational institutions worldwide.

2.4.4 Successful cases of university-industry collaboration

Knowledge is a valued product of universities, which can be proposed to the industry in a corresponding shape as a mover for novel discoveries and innovations. The collaboration between universities and businesses addresses several critical aspects: (a) increasing the role of universities as key actors in the development of knowledge-based economies, (b) utilizing multi-directional relationship marketing for creating partner U-I ties, (c) leveraging digital transformation to establish and strengthen U-I connections, (d) examining the IT's impact on university-enterprise relationship formation, and (e) identifying the key factors necessary for establishing long-term U-I relationships.

Case 1. The authors [56] explore the development of academic and U-I cooperation in AI by analyzing AI 2000, which encompasses domains such as ML, Computer Vision, NLP, IR, Speech Recognition, Knowledge

Engineering, Recommendation Systems, Data Mining, HCI, Multimedia, and others. Among the top 10 universities engaged in the most successful cross-industry collaborations are the Massachusetts Institute of Technology, Carnegie Mellon University, the University of California (Berkeley), the University of Michigan, the University of Washington, Stanford University, the University of Illinois (Urbana-Champaign), Tsinghua University, Columbia University in New York, and the University of Texas at Austin [56]. Among the 10 leading AI companies attracting top scholars over the past few decades are Microsoft, Google, IBM, Intel, Facebook (Meta), Yahoo, Alcatel-Lucent, Hewlett-Packard, Adobe, and Samsung Electronics [56]. Successful AI companies have produced significant research findings in collaboration with university professors and students. For example, 631 universities collaborate with Microsoft, 523 universities with IBM, and 358 universities with Google [56]. It is evident that AI has significantly benefited from cross-industry collaboration in recent decades.

Case 2. Researchers from Hong Kong [57] describe a business datafication project within an e-business course. The project is based on the application of experiential learning methods and supported by U-I partnership to transform the traditional classroom setting by integrating real data, real problems, and real people into the teaching-learning process. In particular, partner companies provided real business data – some of which were confidential – while university students applied this data to experimental studies based on the prioritized tasks that companies needed to solve. CEOs of partner companies actively participated in mentoring students. Through this collaboration, the e-business course was taught using a simulation of real business environments and solving real-world problems. The e-business course allows (a) evolution from off-line learning to fully online data-mining training, (b) transformation from one-university student group projects to joint multi-university projects on a competition basis. The experiences gained from initiating, developing, and implementing this e-business course [57] serve as a model for university-industry collaboration, inspiring educators worldwide to adopt more authentic, relevant, and engaging teaching approaches.

Case 3. It is known, according to geological research, that the Arctic region consists of about 12% of the world's oil and 25% of its gas resources [23]. Shipping companies require experienced and highly skilled personnel to operate ships in Polar Regions. The authors [58] describe a novel digital platform developed in collaboration between three Norwegian institutions (two maritime schools and one university). The joint digital platform was created based on three main components: (a) oil spill preparedness simulator as contribution of the first maritime school; (b) a dynamic positioning simulator for emergency operations (from the second maritime school); and (c) a modern ship bridge simulator (University contribution) with a visual environment, control, command, and other subsystems which are necessary for student training in typical and extremal situations at the open sea, in narrowness, etc. All simulators' systems are cloud-connected and able to be integrated with the different systems of ships including navigation, safety, security, and decision-support. Described joint digital platform allows testing different AI tools for the optimization of marine operations. Key advantages of joint simulation platform include: (a) enabling maritime schools and universities to share costly simulator facilities via the Internet, (b) allowing students and ship crews to conduct joint exercises, in particular, in the framework of search-rescue operations, (c) analyzing student behavior and skills level in emergency response, and (d) facilitating the simulation of various alternative solutions. "Digital twin" technology [23, 59] is used to construct a digital simulation platform that combines simulated data, real-time data, and visualizations.

Other successful cases. The works [8, 32] analyzed successful academic-industry consortia that focused on AI implementation in education processes. Examples are:

- *Arizona State University (ASU) and OpenAI:* A partnership exploring the potentialities of generative AI (ChatGPT) for improving the education sphere, focusing on (a) enhancing student success, (b) fostering innovative research, and (c) streamlining organizational processes.
- *The Simons Foundation and six leading universities in New York:* Established the Empire AI consortium to position New York as a leader in AI implementation. The consortium aims to attract top faculty, expand student educational opportunities, and foster AI-driven startup creation.
- *The Responsible AI UK Consortium:* This initiative unites U-I institutions as UK and international partners to develop responsible and trustworthy AI practices. The consortium also provides for the exchange and sharing of educational resources and knowledge.
- *The Trillion Parameter Consortium:* A global network of researchers from scientific laboratories, research institutes, academia, and industry, working together to address challenges in building large-scale generative AI systems and advancing trustworthy AI for disruptive scientific investigations and discoveries. The National Center for Supercomputing Applications is a founding member.

It is obvious that scientists from universities and the IT industry, who conduct research in an array of fields (computer science, robotics, neuroscience, cognitive science, etc.), must participate in modern AI development and implementation on a partnership basis. Most AI companies have powerful computing facilities for developing, testing, and training modern AI systems. At the same time, for university researchers who don't work at corresponding AI companies [59], accessing powerful AI systems can be limited, difficult, or even impossible. To analyze the scale of activity, it is necessary to take into account that in 2021, the United States government allocated 1.5 billion USD and the European Commission about 1 billion euros (annually) for research and development in the AI field. At the same time, more than 340 billion USD were allocated by AI companies around the world on AI research in 2021. Such a disproportion in the AI financial support underlines the necessity to increase governmental funds for research in the AI field. The Confederation of Laboratories for AI Research in Europe proposed to establish "CERN for AI" [59], focusing on attracting talents in the AI field for creating the most perspective research environment with an orientation on disruptive investigations in the AI field.

Humanity needs the most efficient and reliable AI tools with minimal risks for their practical implementation in education and other areas of human activity. Researchers from different fields of science [60–62] must take part in AI development. All stakeholders must be responsible regarding AI predictability and safety [59]. No doubt, the most efficient results can be obtained when academic and industry scientists develop and control AI tools together.

2.5 Conclusion

This chapter analyzed successful cases of AI integration in educational institutions worldwide, emphasizing the role of digital transformation in enhancing student training at various academic stages.

Special attention was given to international experiences in digital transformation within education systems across developed nations. These insights can accelerate educational reforms in developing countries through the widespread adoption of AI and IT technologies in universities and schools. The study examined best practices from regions including Australia, the United States, Canada, the European Union, Estonia, Finland, France, India, Lithuania, Portugal, the United Kingdom, the Netherlands, Norway, Thailand, and Africa.

The research confirmed the significant role of inter-university collaboration and university-industry partnerships in AI applications within education. Numerous successful examples highlight the benefits of academic and industry alliances in advancing AI-driven education.

Furthermore, the intense competition among AI companies at national and international levels fosters greater efficiency in educational technology. Leading AI companies – including OpenAI, Google, Meta, Microsoft, DeepMind, DeepSeek, and Alibaba – compete to develop advanced AI tools, particularly LLMs, with optimal technical and financial performance. This competitive environment drives the rapid introduction of high-speed, energy-efficient, and cost-effective AI tools into education systems worldwide.

References

[1] Y. Kondratenko, et al., 'Towards Implementing the Strategy of Artificial Intelligence Development: Ukraine Peculiarities,' CEUR Workshop Proceedings, Vol. 3513, 2023, pp. 106–117. https://ceur-ws.org/Vol-3513/paper09.pdf

[2] A.I. Shevchenko, et al., 'Analysis of the prospect domains in AI implementation: Nationals, NATO and Ukraine AI strategies,' in: Y.P. Kondratenko, A.I. Shevchenko (Eds) Research Tendencies and Prospect Domains for AI Development and Implementation, River Publishers, 2024, 1-30. https://www.riverpublishers.com/book_details.php?book_id=1163

[3] J. Kacprzyk, et al., 'A Fuzzy Multistage Control Model for Stable Sustainable Agricultural Regional Development', in: P. Shi, et al. (eds) Complex Systems: Spanning Control and Computational Cybernetics: Foundations, Studies in Systems, Decision and Control, Springer, Cham, Vol. 415, 2022, pp. 299–329. DOI:10.1007/978-3-031-00978-5_13

[4] Y. Kondratenko, et al., 'Analysis of the Priorities and Perspectives in Artificial Intelligence Implementation,' 2023 13th International Conference on Dependable Systems, Services and Technologies, DESSERT 2023, 2023, Athens, 13 – 15 October 2023, DOI10.1109/DESSERT61349.2023.10416432

[5] J. Kacprzyk, et al., 'A Status Quo Biased Multistage Decision Model for Regional Agricultural Socioeconomic Planning Under Fuzzy Information,' in: Y.P. Kondratenko, et al. (Eds) Advanced Control Techniques in Complex Engineering Systems: Theory and Applications, Studies in

Systems, Decision and Control, Vol. 203, Springer, Cham, 2019, pp. 201-226. https://doi.org/10.1007/978-3-030-21927-7_10

[6] J. Kacprzyk, et al., 'A Fuzzy Multistage Control Model for Sustainable Regional Agricultural Development: Effectiveness and Stability,' In: J. Hernández, et al. (eds.), Agriculture Value Chain—Challenges and Trends in Academia and Industry, Studies in Systems, Decision and Control, Vol. 557, Springer, Cham, 2025, pp. 253-281. https://doi.org/10.1007/978-3-031-70745-2_17

[7] R. Duro, et al. (Eds), 'Advances in intelligent robotics and collaborative automation,' River Publishers, Aalborg, 2015. DOI:https://doi.org/10.13052/rp-9788793237049

[8] Y.P. Kondratenko, V.I. Slyusar, M.B. Solesvik, N.Y. Kondratenko, Z. Gomolka, 'Interrelation and inter-influence of artificial intelligence and higher education systems,' in: Y. Kondratenko, et al. (Eds) Research Tendencies and Prospect Domains for AI Development and Implementation, 2024, pp. 31–58. https://www.scopus.com/record/display.uri?eid=2-s2.0-85202992102&origin=resultslist

[9] V. Slyusar, et al., 'Some Aspects of Artificial Intelligence Development Strategy for Mobile Technologies,' Journal of Mobile Multimedia, Vol. 20, Iss. 03, 2024, pp. 525–554. https://doi.org/10.13052/jmm1550 4646.2031

[10] F. Gabriel, et al., 'Digital education strategies around the world: practices and policies,' Irish Educational Studies, Volume 41, No. 1, 2022, pp. 85–106. https://doi.org/10.1080/03323315.2021.2022513

[11] Z. Gomolka, et al., 'Diagnosing Dyslexia in Early School-Aged Children Using the LSTM Network and Eye Tracking Technology,' Applied Sciences (Switzerland), 2024, 14(17), 8004. https://doi.org/10.3390/app14178004

[12] F.J. Cantú-Ortiz, et al., 'An artificial intelligence educational strategy for the digital transformation,' International Journal on Interactive Design and Manufacturing, Vol. 14, 2020, pp.1195–1209. https://doi.org/10.1007/s12008-020-00702-8

[13] Y. Kondratenko, D. Simon, I. Atamanyuk, 'University Curricula Modification Based on Advancements in Information and Communication Technologies,' CEUR Workshop Proceedings, Vol. 1614, 2016, pp. 184–199. https://ceur-ws.org/Vol-1614/paper_18.pdf

[14] B. Collis, J. Moonen, 'Flexible learning in a digital world: experiences and expectations,' Routledge, Taylor & Francis Group, London and New York, 2001.

[15] A. Bhutoria, 'Personalized Education and Artificial Intelligence in the United States, China, and India: A Systematic Review Using a Human-In-The-Loop Model,' Computers and Education: Artificial Intelligence, Volume 3, 2022, 100068.

[16] M. Tetyana, Y. Kondratenko, I. Sidenko, G. Kondratenko, 'Computer Vision Mobile System for Education Using Augmented Reality Technology,' Journal of Mobile Multimedia, Vol. 17, Is. 4, 2021, pp. 555-576. DOI:10.13052/jmm1550-4646.1744

[17] A. Jaiswal, et al., 'Potential of Artificial Intelligence for transformation of the education system in India,' Intern. Journal of Education and Development using Information and Communication Technology (IJEDICT), Vol. 17, Issue 1, 2021, pp. 142-158.

[18] T. Wang, et al., 'Exploring the Potential Impact of Artificial Intelligence (AI) on International Students in Higher Education: Generative AI, Chatbots, Analytics, and International Student Success,' Applied Sciences, Vol. 13(11), 2023, 6716.

[19] F. Pedro, et al., 'Artificial Intelligence in Education: Challenges and Opportunities for Sustainable Development,' Education 2030, Working Papers on Education Policy 7, United Nations Educational, Scientific and Cultural Organization, Paris, 2019.

[20] G. Kondratenko, et al., 'Fuzzy Decision Making System for Model-Oriented Academia/Industry Cooperation: University Preferences', in: C. Berger-Vachon, et al. (Eds) Complex Systems: Solutions and Challenges in Economics, Management and Engineering, Studies in Systems, Decision and Control, Vol. 125, Springer, Cham, 2018, pp. 109-124. https://doi.org/10.1007/978-3-319-69989-9_7

[21] Y. Kondratenko, et al., 'Intelligent Decision Support System for Selecting the University-Industry Cooperation Model Using Modified Antecedent-Consequent Method,' in: J. Medina et al. (Eds) Information Processing and Management of Uncertainty in Knowledge-Based Systems: Theory and Foundations, IPMU 2018, Communications in Computer and Information Science, Vol. 854. Springer, Cham. 2018, pp. 596–607. https://doi.org/10.1007/978-3-319-91476-3_49

[22] Y.P. Kondratenko, et al., 'Knowledge-Based Decision Support System with Reconfiguration of Fuzzy Rule Base for Model-Oriented Academic-Industry Interaction', in: A.M. Gil-Lafuente, et al. (eds.), Applied Mathematics and Computational Intelligence, FIM 2015, Advances in Intelligent Systems and Computing, Vol. 730, Springer, Cham, 2018, pp. 101-112. https://doi.org/10.1007/978-3-319-7579 2-6_9

[23] M. Solesvik, et al., ‘Architecture for Collaborative Digital Simulation for the Polar Regions’, in: V. Kharchenko, et al. (eds), Green IT Engineering: Social, Business and Industrial Applications, Studies in Systems, Decision and Control, Vol. 171, Springer, Cham, pp. 517-531, 2019. DOI: https://doi.org/10.1007/978-3-030-00253-4_22

[24] C. Linse, et al., ‘Education Infrastructure for Inter-organizational University Collaborations,’ SEFI Journal of Engineering Education Advancement, Vol. 1(1), 2024, pp. 53–79. https://doi.org/10.62492/sefijeea.v1i1.16

[25] Y. Du, et al., ’Research on innovation cooperation network of Chinese universities based on patent data,’ Journal of Engineering and Technology Management, Volume 71, 2024, 101784, ISSN 0923-4748. https://doi.org/10.1016/j.jengtecman.2023.101784.

[26] Zhou Zhong, et al., ’Universities as cities of flows: decoding cross-regional university partnerships for sustainable development in China’, Int. Journal of Comparative Education and Development, Vol. 26, Is. 3, 2024, pp. 208 – 225. DOI:10.1108/IJCED-08-2023-0075

[27] V. Fedák, et al., ‘Best Practice for Boosting Innovation in the HEI through the Initiative of European University Alliances,’ 20th Intern. Conf. on Emerging eLearning Technologies and Applications (ICETA), Stary Smokovec, Slovakia, 2022, pp. 153-158. DOI:10.1109/ICETA57911.2022.9974895

[28] A. Tibaut, et al., ‘Inter-university Virtual Learning Environment,’ in: M. Ivanović, et al. (Eds) E-Learning Paradigms and Applications, Studies in Computational Intelligence, Vol. 528, Springer, Berlin, Heidelberg, 2014, pp. 97–119.

[29] R. Poceviciene, ’University alliances as an educational environment for higher quality education: aspect of development and implementation of European values,’ ICERI-2024 Proceedings, 2024, pp. 3810-3816. DOI: 10.21125/iceri.2024.0963

[30] Y. Hou, et al., ‘Training future professors in public budgeting, finance, and financial management: The Inter-University Consortium for PhD courses,’ Journal of Public Affairs Education, Vol. 30(3), 2023, pp. 375–394. https://doi.org/10.1080/15236803.2023.2272654

[31] X. Yang, et al., ‘Advancing digital transformation in TVET through international cooperation: Approaches by the UNESCO Chair on Digitalization in TVET,’ Vocat Tech Edu, Vol. 1(2), 2024. DOI:10.54844/vte.2024.0585

[32] Y.P. Kondratenko, A.I Shevchenko (Eds), 'Research Tendencies and Prospect Domains for AI Development and Implementation', River Publishers, 2024, pp. 1–155. https://www.riverpublishers.com/book_details.php?book_id=1163,ISBN978-877004692-3
[33] L. Zenkienė, et al., 'Strengthening university capacity in regional innovation ecosystem through the participation in the European Universities initiative,' European Journal of Higher Education, 14(sup1), 2024, pp. 88–108.
[34] L. Eutsler, et al., 'A self-study of an inter-university partnership to integrate technology into instruction,' Technology, Pedagogy and Education, Vol. 32(5), 2023, pp. 569–588. https://doi.org/10.1080/1475939X.2023.2246983
[35] X. Wang, et al., 'The Development of Legal Education in the Context of Enabling Artificial Intelligence,' Journal of Advanced Research in Social and Behavioural Sciences, Vol. 38, Issue 1, 2025, pp. 27-41. https://doi.org/10.37934/jarsbs.38.1.2741
[36] Y. Kondratenko, et al. 'Tendencies and Challenges of Artificial Intelligence Development and Implementation,' in: IDAACS'2023 Proceedings, Vol. 1, 2023, pp. 221-226. DOI:10.1109/IDAACS58523.2023.10348800
[37] V. Shebanin, et al., 'Development of the Mathematical Model of the Informational Resource of a Distance Learning System', in: O. Chertov, et al. (eds.), Recent Developments in Data Science and Intelligent Analysis of Information, ICDSIAI 2018 Proceedings, Advances in Intelligent Systems and Computing, Vol. 836, Springer, Cham, 2019, pp. 199-205. DOI:10.1007/978-3-319-97885-7_20
[38] V. Shebanin, et al., 'Application of Fuzzy Predicates and Quantifiers by Matrix Presentation in Informational Resources Modeling', Perspective Technologies and Methods in MEMS Design: MEMSTECH-2016 Proceedings, Lviv-Poljana, Ukraine, April 20-24, 2016, pp. 146-149. DOI:10.1109/MEMSTECH.2016.7507536
[39] D. Castelvecchi, 'META Creates AI Translator for Dozens of Languages,' Nature, Vol. 637, 23 January 2025, pp. 771-772.
[40] AlphaSignal. https://alphasignal.ai/example
[41] Introducing Eureka Labs. https://eurekalabs.ai/
[42] M. Dempsey, 'Future data centres may have built-in nuclear reactors,' BBC, 14 February 2024. https://www.bbc.com/news/business-68238330

[43] M. Terrell, 'New nuclear clean energy agreement with Kairos Power,' The Keyword, Google, 14 October 2024. https://blog.google/outreach-initiatives/sustainability/google-kairos-power-nuclear-energy-agreement/
[44] D. Castelvecchi, 'Will AI's huge energy demands spur a nuclear renaissance?' Nature, Vol. 635, 7 November 2024, pp. 19-20.
[45] G. Conroy, S. Mallapaty, 'How China created AI model DeepSeek and shocked the world,' Nature, Vol. 638, 13 February 2025, pp. 300-301.
[46] Sujita Sinha, 'Trump plans $500 billion AI power to defeat diseases, enemies at 'unprecedented' rate,' Blueprint, Interesting Engineering, January 22, 2025. https://interestingengineering.com
[47] Ameya Paleja, 'DeepSeek: China's cheap AI melts NVIDIA's $600 billion, tanks $1 trillion from US tech,' Blueprint, Interesting Engineering, January 28, 2025. https://interestingengineering.com
[48] Sarah Parvin, 'Chinese tech startup DeepSeek says it was hit with 'large-scale malicious attacks,' AP, January 27, 2025. https://apnews.com/article/deepseek-ai-artificial-intelligence-be414acadbf35070d7645fe9fbd8f464
[49] Joshua Hawkins, 'Researchers recreated DeepSeek's core technology for just $30,' BGR, January 29, 2025. https://bgr.com/tech/researchers-recreated-deepseeks-core-technology-for-just-30/?_bhlid=0b8c7ae7553075d463e897c86252626f76faead9
[50] E. Gibney, 'China's cheap, open AI model DeepSeek thrills scientists,' Nature, Vol. 638, 6 February 2025, pp. 13-14.
[51] Heather Long, 'Drill, baby, drill' is hitting a pricing problem,' Washington Post, January 30, 2025. https://www.washingtonpost.com
[52] 'Qwen2.5-Max: Exploring the Intelligence of Large-scale MoE Model,' Qwen Team, January 28, 2025. https://qwenlm.github.io/blog/qwen2.5-max/
[53] E. Baptista, 'Alibaba releases AI model it says surpasses DeepSeek,' Reuters, January 29, 2025. https://www.reuters.com/technology/artificial-intelligence/alibaba-releases-ai-model-it-claims-surpasses-deepseek-v3-2025-01-29/
[54] S. Sinha, 'Grok 3: Elon Musk unleashes 'smartest AI on Earth,' claims it beats Google, OpenAI,' Interesting Engineering, 18 February 2025. https://interestingengineering.com/culture/elon-musk-unveils-grok-3-ai

[55] M. Lis, 'Higher Education Institutions and Digital Transformation: Building University-Enterprise Collaborative Relationships,' Routledge, Taylor & Francis, 2023.

[56] Z. Shao, et al., 'Institutional Collaboration and Competition in Artificial Intelligence,' in: IEEE Access, Vol. 8, pp. 69734-69741, 2020.

[57] R.C-W. Kwok, et al., 'Business Datafication Project for Intrapreneurship Supported by University-Industry Collaboration,' In: Int. Journal of Innovative Business Strategies, Vol. 10, No. 2, 2024, pp. 737-744. https://doi.org/10.20533/ijibs.2046.3626.2024.0090

[58] M. Solesvik, et al., 'Joint Digital Simulation Platforms for Safety and Preparedness', in: Y. Luo (ed), Cooperative Design, Visualization, and Engineering, CDVE 2018, Lecture Notes in Computer Science, vol. 11151, Springer, Cham, pp. 118-125, 2018. https://doi.org/10.1007/978-3-030-00560-3_16

[59] Editorial, 'How to prepare for more-powerful AI,' Nature, 636, 12 Dec. 2024, 273.

[60] I. P. Atamanyuk, et al., 'The Algorithm of Optimal Polynomial Extrapolation of Random Processes,' in: K.J. Engemann, et al. (Eds.) Modeling and Simulation in Engineering, Economics and Management, Lecture Notes in Business Information Processing, Vol. 115, Springer, 2012, pp. 78-87. DOI:10.1007/978-3-642-30433-0_9

[61] Y.P. Kondratenko, et al., 'Slip displacement sensors for intelligent robots: Solutions and models,' Proc. 2013 IEEE 7th International Conference on Intelligent Data Acquisition and Advanced Computing Systems, IDAACS 2013, 2, pp. 861–866, 6663050, 2013. DOI:10.1109/IDAACS.2013.6663050

[62] Y.P. Kondratenko, et al., 'Parametric optimization of fuzzy control systems based on hybrid particle swarm algorithms with elite strategy,' Journal of Automation and Information Sciences 51(12), pp. 25-45, 2019. DOI:10.1615/JAutomatInfScien.v51.i12.40

3

AI and Digital Evolution in the Education System of Ukraine

Y.P. Kondratenko[1,2], Y.D. Zhukov[3,5,7], A.I. Shevchenko[2], O.Y. Zhukova[3,6,7], and O.S. Striuk[1,4]

[1]Petro Mohyla Black Sea National University, Ukraine
[2]Institute of Artificial Intelligence Problems, Ukraine
[3]National University of Shipbuilding, Ukraine
[4]University of Ostrava, Czech Republic
[5]C-Job Nikolayev, Ukraine
[6]MDEM, Ukraine
[7]AMICO, Ukraine
E-mail: rcktor_iai@ukr.nct; y_kondrat2002@yahoo.com; prof.zhukov@gmail.com; eyzhukova@gmail.com; oleksandr.striuk@gmail.com

Abstract

This chapter discusses the current state of digital transformation and artificial intelligence (AI) introduced in the Ukrainian education system. Among the focuses are STEM education, SMART technologies, online education and the experience of the leading Ukrainian universities in creating neural networks' ML-laboratory, "Internet of Things" specialization, research laboratory of mechatronics and robotics, innovation ecosystem Sikorsky Challenge, and others. Special attention is paid to (a) innovating shipbuilding education in Ukraine; (b) the development of international academia-business collaboration in navigating Shipbuilding 4.0; (c) analysis of the successful cases and perspectives of AI application in the Ukrainian education system; and (d) peculiarities of its post-war recovery.

Keywords: AI, digital transformation, education, successful cases, shipbuilding education.

DOI: 10.1201/9788743809258-3

3.1 Introduction

Today, artificial intelligence (AI) plays a significant role in society's development [1–6]. Ukraine actively provides a digital transformation of its education system and introduces modern AI tools to increase the efficiency of the learning and teaching processes [7, 8]. Ukrainian universities have many partners abroad among well-known universities and companies and provide improving the educational processes within academia consortia and university-business collaboration. Ukraine needs highly qualified graduates who can help the country in post-war recovery.

The main goal of this chapter is to analyze the successful cases of digital transformation and AI use in the Ukrainian education system based on the experience of leading Ukrainian universities, inter-institutional collaboration, and academia-business cooperation with a special focus on innovative shipbuilding education.

The rest of the chapter is organized as follows. Section 3.2 discusses successful cases of digital transformation and AI tools introductions in the education system of Ukraine focusing (a) on creating neural networks' ML-laboratory, "Internet of Things" specialization, research laboratory of mechatronics and robotics, innovation ecosystem Sikorsky Challenge and (b) on analysis of successful students' research and publications in the framework inter-university cooperation on the domestic and international level. The perspective approaches in innovating shipbuilding education in Ukraine and peculiarities of the development of international academia-business collaboration in navigating Shipbuilding 4.0 are discussed in Section 3.3. Section 3.4 concludes the chapter.

3.2 Digital Evolution and AI Implementation in the Education System of Ukraine: Successful Cases

Improving the quality of education processes in Ukraine involves expanding the implementation of advanced information technologies (IT) and AI tools in the education system, while meeting the informational needs of universities and schools. This approach allows the creation of a single-digitized platform for the university, using modern methods of information interaction and universal teaching-learning tools with corresponding tracking of all changes in the dynamics of the information environment and with necessary interactive corrections. Figure 3.1 illustrates the rise (%) of the level of information systems (IS) implementation in the education system of Ukraine during the 2020-2023 period [9].

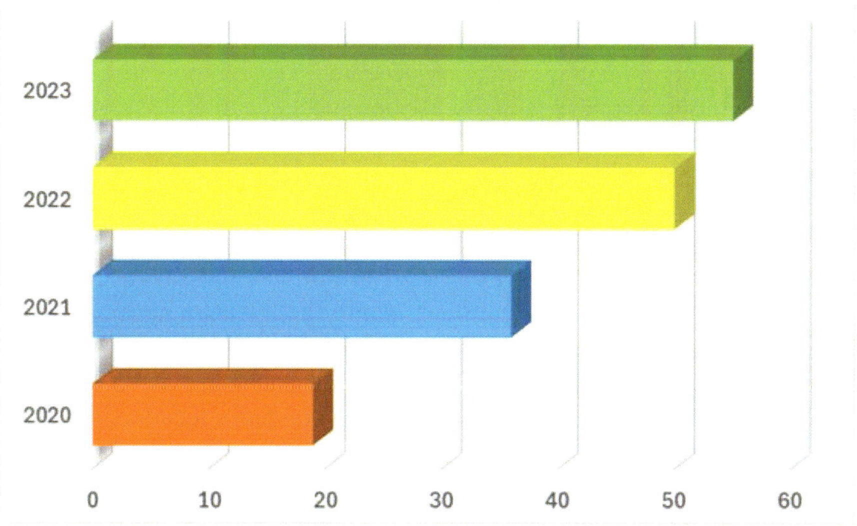

Figure 3.1 Implementation of IS in the education environment.

The study [10] underlines the significance of embracing educational innovation and digital transformation in the Ukrainian education system and the wide potential of digital technologies to enhance teaching and learning processes, improve training results, and support socio-economic development. Among the main innovative digital technologies in the educational system [9] are AI, IT, computer technologies, interactive learning, augmented (AR) and virtual reality (VR), hybrid cloud technologies, mobile technologies, multimedia technologies, portal technologies, and others. Based on successful foreign experience, Ukraine can accelerate the implementation of relevant digital and innovative solutions in its own educational conception [9]. The formation of professional competence in future specialists is defined by communicative, intercultural, and informational-digital competence, considering the trend of integrating the educational space into the European community. Innovative digitalization technologies, including immersive tools, virtual reality instruments, and AI, are particularly effective in forming the critical competencies of higher education students in conditions close to professional activity realities.

The successful integration of AI tools in higher education requires careful consideration of stakeholders' attitudes toward such introduction processes. Stakeholders [9] (students and their parents, faculty members, administrators, alumni, future employers of graduates, and policymakers) play an important role in the choice and evaluation of introduced AI tools. The study [11] analyzes stakeholders' opinions concerning AI methods and tools in Ukrainian universities through expert group discussions and a quantitative survey questionnaire of external participants. The experts noted the efficient impact of AI integration on the education process, focusing on success for personalized learning and real-time student-teacher feedback but also underlined that, in some cases, the AI-generated content has non-high accuracy.

Many innovative methods are applied in the Ukrainian education system, including project-based learning, inquiry-based learning, case-study approach, collaborative learning, peer learning, simulations, gamification, distance learning, blended learning, AI-supported teaching, and VR [12–14]. Let us consider using some innovations in the Ukrainian education system.

STEM education. Innovative techniques bring certain advantages to STEM (science, technology, engineering, and mathematics) education and enhance the process of training future STEM professionals. The authors of a study [14] present the effective organization of STEM-based curricula within Ukrainian educational institutions and describe helping to reduce education costs, increase access to education, make the educational process more interactive, organize professional development for teachers, and prepare students to solve real-world tasks.

Online education. Online education provides the choice of courses or learning materials according to the students' desires and aspirations promoting learning at their personal time and own pace. During the COVID-19 pandemic and the Russian-Ukrainian war online education played a significant role in increasing the efficiency of the education system of Ukraine. Since the introduction of online learning, there are no longer any physical, transportation, or geographic limitations or obstacles to teaching-learning processes in Ukrainian schools and universities. It allows Ukrainian students to access education regardless of their location, age, or social status [15] using main learning platforms such as Zoom – 70.13%, Microsoft Teams – 16.88%, and Google Meet – 12.99% and organizational platforms such as Moodle – 54.55%, Google Classroom – 36.06%, and others – 10.39%.

SMART technologies. Modern SMART technologies play a significant role in the Ukrainian language's learning process due to their multimedia nature. They compensate for the lack of a real language environment by providing virtual linguistic and extra-linguistic visibility. Exploring SMART technologies in teaching the Ukrainian language to students in general secondary and higher education institutions and conducting comparative and content analysis of distance and electronic learning are discussed in a study [16]. The authors emphasize the effectiveness of using (a) interactive whiteboards and (b) multimedia presentations to implement the principle of visualizing language elements and structures and (c) creating mental maps as an effective SMART teaching technology for the Ukrainian language based on computer services such as MindMeister, Mindomo, Cliffy, Spinscape, Bubbl.us, MAP-MYself, SpiderScribe, and others. Among the main directions for learning the Ukrainian language are: (a) Ukrainian language for philological specialties; (b) professional-oriented Ukrainian language; (c) Ukrainian language for foreign students. One of the forms of SMART learning is a virtual learning environment, which was created, in particular, at Lviv Polytechnic National University [16] for daily use with various forms of control and self-control of the student's learning achievements and contains all the necessary elements of theoretical and practical knowledge. The virtual learning environment is created for both (a) managing the learning process in distance learning, and (b) supporting online learning with an emphasis on the learning process itself.

Digital trends in education. Among the major digital trends for the development of Society 5.0 and the formation of graduates' competencies required for Industry 4.0 are [17]:

- *AI technologies* (modern functionality of AI and machine learning (ML) tools used for speech, gesture and image recognition, medical and technical diagnostics, content and financial analysis, document management, spam detection, etc.);
- *Internet of Things* (smart equipment, intelligent cars and offices, smart homes, smart cities and more);
- *Robotic technologies for process automation* (application of robotics in manufacturing, trade, transport, healthcare, rescue work, education, agriculture, and military affairs in the form of cobots, drones, mobile, and medical robots);
- *Big Data* (structured or unstructured datasets of large volume are characterized by volume, velocity, variety, veracity, variability, and value and are used for statistics, analysis, forecasting, and decision-making).

Ukrainian university graduates to succeed in their future working careers must be able to apply the theoretical knowledge and practical skills obtained in neural networks, ML, fuzzy logic, intelligent robotics, sensors, computer vision, pattern recognition, natural language processing (NLP), applied software, communication technologies, etc.

The Ministry of Digital Transformation of Ukraine has developed a catalog [18] of educational programs for applicants with information about the training specialists in AI.

The following digital technologies of AI education are recommended [19] for use in Ukrainian universities: Edtech, edutainment, intelligent tutoring system (ITS), cloud technology, ML, NLP, smart content, VR/AR, computer vision, intelligent adaptive learning, vision and voice applications, digital skills, AI-driven education ecosystem, AI-powered chatbot, AI-powered virtual assistants, fraud and risk management, learning platform and virtual facilitators, e-learning, automated assessment and grading tasks, personalized education. The recommendations [19] may be applied to develop national AI standards to improve the educational system that trains competent specialists.

Determining the level of teachers' satisfaction and identifying the main problems and advantages of using AI in Ukrainian schools are reflected in a study [20]. A survey conducted among 807 respondents in December 2023 showed that (a) the most popular services are ChatGPT and Bard and (b) the main AI advantages deal with increasing the availability of materials, improving the organization of the educational process, and automating the creation of didactic material. At the same time, the main disadvantages deal with technical limitations and risks associated with excessive dependence on AI technology.

IT industry of Ukraine in 2020 included 20 regional IT clusters, 8 IT associations, 10 IT Incubators and IT accelerators, 50 HUBs, 19 venture funds, four technology parks, and more than 100 R&D centers [17, 21]. In addition, many co-working spaces serve as development centers for young startups. However, these ecosystems, involving the best young Ukrainian talents in the vast majority work not for Ukrainian customers but for global markets.

Let us discuss several successful cases of digital transformations and AI implementations in the Ukrainian education system [17, 22,23,24, 25–28].

Case 1. Within the Global Logic Education initiative framework, based on the Faculty of Computer Science and Cybernetics of the Taras Shevchenko National University of Kyiv, a master's program of dual education in AI was introduced and an educational ML-laboratory of neural networks was opened. The most common products being developed in this lab are virtual voice assistants, search engines, chatbots, and video surveillance systems for crime prevention. Masters and graduates have an excellent opportunity to gain practical skills in software development and conduct postgraduate studies under the guidance of experienced company employees.

Case 2. "Internet of Things" specialization at Lviv Polytechnic University, which was created on the initiative of the Lviv IT Cluster, is an example of successful cooperation between Ukrainian universities and the IT industry. As a result, the students acquire knowledge and skills in IoT security, cloud computing, data analysis, automation, embedded systems, M2M technologies, machine learning, and the like.

Case 3. The research laboratory of mechatronics and robotics of the Odesa National Academy of Food Technologies, based on which the south training center of the Italian company Camozzi, a leading global manufacturer of industrial pneumatics, was created, is an example of successful cooperation between Ukrainian universities and foreign companies in the field of robotics. The laboratory has become a full member of the Association of Robotics of Ukraine, which gives it the right to participate in international competitions among portable robotic systems with AI.

Case 4. The Kyiv Smart City team, the Socrat STEM center, and the 2D3D Distribution LLC as technical partner have created the First League of Technical Challenges in Ukraine to hold a robotics competition to increase the interest of young people in the exact sciences and modern AI technologies [17].

Case 5. The innovation ecosystem "Sikorsky Challenge" implements the full technological cycle of innovative entrepreneurship: from searching for new ideas to attracting investments to create innovative products. The Sikorsky Challenge startup school established at the Igor Sikorsky Kyiv Polytechnic Institute is the first innovation ecosystem created based on a university in Ukraine [22]. Innovation Ecosystem Sikorsky Challenge covers a startup school, business incubator, festival of innovation projects, an innovative technological environment named "Sikorsky Lab," a center for intellectual property, and a venture fund. Since 2012, more than 100 projects presented at the Sikorsky Challenge have received investment support. The final competition of innovative projects in 2021 was held in six sections: (1) IT, digital country, and cybersecurity;(2) defense and security; (3) industrial high-tech and space; (4) green energy and ecology; (5) biomedical engineering and human health; and (6) agricultural engineering.

Case 6. The SoftServe University created by the IT Company SoftServe [23] in cooperation with the Lviv Polytechnic University can be represented as the educational ecosystem. The SoftServe University includes [17]:

- talent development center for talented people who are beginning their career in IT;

- business school for the advancement of leadership and management competencies;
- technology school for the development of technical skills and competencies;
- intercultural communication center;
- certification center from Microsoft, Oracle, PMI, Amazon, Salesforce, and iSQI;
- training excellence center for teaching management based on international trends.

SoftServe University's activity in 2022 led to 11,298 unique educational solutions, 13,870 internal training program participants, and 6000+ external trailing program participants.

Case 7. The good educational practices in the AI field are the cooperation between students and teachers of BSNU (Petro Mohyla Black Sea National University, Mykolaiv, Ukraine), NUOS (Admiral Makarov National University of Shipbuilding, Mykolaiv, Ukraine), CSU (Cleveland State University, Cleveland, Ohio, USA), SU (Saarland University, Saarbrucken, Germany) and USC (University of South Carolina, Colombia, SC, USA). Student/teacher collaboration allows students to be involved in active AI research, scientific presentations, and high-caliber publications by developing new AI-based systems for different real-world applications in the framework of each training step's projects (research, undergraduate and graduate diploma, courses) and PhD thesis. In particular, students have practiced oral and online presentations at the annual All-Ukrainian Scientific Conference (https://dspace.chmnu.edu.ua/jspui/handle/123456789/2631) "Intelligent Information Systems," BSNU, Mykolaiv. Selected successful cases of joint student/teacher published results, which are included in the scientific database Scopus, based on collaboration between scientists and students of BSNU, CSU, SU, USC, and NUOS are presented in Table 3.1.

Case 8. The methodology of AI tools introduction to Ukrainian universities is described in a study [62] based on the analysis of used AI in teaching and learning processes at the National University "Lviv Polytechnic," National Technical University "Kharkiv Polytechnic University," the State University of Telecommunications, Igor Sikorsky National University "Kyiv Polytechnic Institute," and National Aviation University (now State University "Kyiv Aviation Institute"). The research team included 42 instructors from these universities who represented graduating departments that (a) were responsible for the development of educational and professional programs, (b) formulated the training objectives, and (c) designed

Table 3.1 Selected publications by students as co-authors (Scopus)

No.	The research topic in "student-teacher" collaboration	Student's Name	University	Reference
1	Diagnosis of lung disease based on medical images using neural networks	A. Sheremet	BSNU	[25]
2	Artificial neural networks for recognition of brain tumors on MRI images	V. Petrovich, I. Sova, M. Taranov	BSNU	[26, 27]
3	Neuro-fuzzy observers of clamping force for magnetically operated mobile robots	O. Gerasin	NUOS	[28]
4	ML algorithms for binary classification of liver disease	A. Sokoliuk	BSNU	[29]
5	Information, communication, and modeling technologies in prosthetic leg and robotics research at Cleveland State University	G. Khademi, V. Azimi, D. Ebeigbe, M. Abdelhady, S. Fakoorian, T. Barto, A.Y. Roshanineshat	CSU	[30, 31]
6	IoT-complex for analysis and monitoring of motor highway conditions	R.Leizerovych	BSNU	[32]
7	AI in an automated system for web-interfaces visual testing	K. Ivanova	BSNU	[33]
8	Scoring system based on neural networks for image perception	I. Khortiuk	BSNU	[34]
9	Mobile recognition of image components based on ML methods	M. Saliutin	BSNU	[35]
10	Neural technologies for objects classification with mobile applications	O. Heras	BSNU	[36]
11	Hybrid fuzzy-color computing based on optical logical architecture	V. Horbov	NUOS	[37]
12	Soft computing analytic models, real-time fuzzy data processing	N. Kondratenko	USC	[38–44]
13	Computer vision system for education using AR technologies	Tetyana Misyuk	BSNU	[12]
14	ML for the robot's sensor and control information processing	S. Sichevskyi	BSNU	[45, 46]
15	Computerized intelligent system for remote diagnostics	A. Topalov	NUOS	[47]
16	Intelligent forecasting system for NPP's energy production	O. Chornovol	BSNU	[48]

Table 3.1 *Continued.*

No.	The research topic in "student-teacher" collaboration	Student's Name	University	Reference
17	Simulation of robot's wheel-mover on ferromagnetic surfaces	C. Wolf, N. Taranov	SU, BSNU	[49]
18	Neural network for recognizing military objects on satellite images	O. Kovaliv	BSNU	[50]
19	Optimization of fuzzy systems, hybrid gray wolf algorithms, intelligent control	O. Skakodub	BSNU	[51–53]
20	GAN for creating photorealistic images and fingerprint samples	O. Striuk	BSNU	[54, 55]
21	Advanced approaches to reduce the number of actors in a magnetically-operated wheel-mover of a mobile robot	C. Wolf, N. Taranov, O. Gerasin	SU, BSNU, NUOS	[56]
22	Modification of the fuzzy TOPSIS method	D. Hapishko	BSNU	[57]
23	A simulation model for the robot's slip displacement sensors	O. Gerasin, A. Topalov	NUOS	[58]
24	ML for UAV routing on rough terrain	A. Trukhov	BSNU	[59]
25	Eye-tracking technology for the analysis of dynamic data	K. Filina, D. Chabanovskyi	BSNU	[60]
26	Neural networks for adaptive control system on FPGA	E. Gordienko	NUOS	[61]

the conceptual framework for the creation of an innovative educational environment with the use of AI. The research resulted in the development of methodical recommendations for applying teaching methods and approaches in AI-powered higher education.

Post-war recovery of Ukraine and its education. Russia's full-scale invasion of Ukraine leads to the systematic destruction of Ukraine's education system. Hundreds of schools have been destroyed, with teachers, students, and parents killed due to Russia's military aggression. The education of millions of children has been interrupted and the continuity of teaching and learning continues to be a struggle.

The publication [63] states that countries participating in the OECD program on the Future of Education and Skills (Education 2030) offer a range of case studies on how they have tackled major educational challenges and transformed learning and schooling following significant disruptions. They offer a variety of policy ideas and implementation examples that may benefit Ukrainian educators and policymakers as they strive to sustain and transform learning, teaching, and schooling in Ukraine. The experienced authors represent India, Estonia, Finland, Ireland, Japan, Korea, Canada, and Portugal.

Integral assessment of the security situation in the Ukrainian education system under the intensive implementation of artificial intelligence technologies and identification of promising scenarios for the post-war reconstruction of Ukraine are discussed in a study [64]. The module of intelligent economic-mathematical modeling and forecasting of scenarios for the implementation of digital initiatives for the post-war recovery of the educational system of Ukraine is realized based on IBM SPSS Modeler, AI-Prophet, Cloud Pak for Data, and R-Studio AI. Based on the obtained integrated assessment of the security of the educational system [64], the authors have identified probable trajectories for the transformation of educational processes in the context of the use of AI technologies. Key scenarios for the improvement of tactical and strategic management tools in the education sector are proposed to accelerate the processes of high-quality digital transformation aimed at the post-war recovery of Ukraine.

3.3 AI's Role in Innovating Shipbuilding Education

3.3.1 Drivers and challenges of Ukrainian ship engineering education

Historically known for its robust shipbuilding capabilities, Ukraine started intensively integrating contemporary technologies, particularly into ship design and engineering, at the end of the 20th century. This process was the cornerstone of integration into the European and global shipbuilding supply chains, attracting foreign investment in cooperation with shipyards and engineering offices.

Internal Reskilling/Upskilling Model (IRUM) in Ukraine (2003-2009). The rapid advancement of integration began with the arrival of a strategic investor, the Dutch Damen Group, at the Ocean Shipyard in Mykolaiv at the end of the last century. Ship Design & Engineering Ukraine (SDEU) LLC was established in 2003 in response to the need for modernization. This company focuses on integrating modern methods and digital tools to address the shortage of local engineers with contemporary expertise. A simplified model of internal apprenticeship of rather skilled engineers allowed an increase in the SDEU staff capacity to nearly triple. The retraining program was designed for one month of full-time training on using essential tools of leading naval CAD solutions, followed by one and a half months of practice at one of Damen Shipyard Ocean to study the specifics of technological processes and equipment capabilities that considerably influence engineering processes.

After new employees complete this program, the company could add them to the project teams and sell their hours at the appropriate initial rates. By 2006, the above strategy had increased the share of exports in SDEU products to 80%. The quality and efficiency of the projects had reached the European level. It was a real success story as, at that time, there were enough qualified middle-aged engineers with sufficient expertise in shipbuilding and other high-tech engineering industries. To address this issue, the management at SDEU began implementing "Summer practices" for senior undergraduate students from Admiral Makarov National University of Shipbuilding. These students were temporarily employed part-time to gain foundational skills in the 3D modeling of simple structural and mechanical components of ships. This experience was intended to create a pool of prepared employees for future needs. Many of these students continue to work as freelancers while pursuing their master's degrees to maintain their expertise. Moreover, the inherited model of internal apprenticeship at SDEU requires significant enhancement and scaling up of the entire curriculum, including training for other digital solutions and software packages.

The subsequent dynamic period of development of the IRUM model continued for another three years, from 2006 to 2009, after Damen Shipyards OKEAN and SDEU were sold to AKER Yards Group, one of the largest corporations in European shipbuilding, based in Oslo, Norway. This group was focused on much larger and more complicated vessels, using more diversified CAD/CAM/CAE systems and utilizing distributed ship design and engineering processes in time and locations. SDEU was renamed to Aker Yards Design Ukraine (AYDU), but it was not only rebranding. The significant changes in the types and sizes of vessels designed and constructed by AKER, along with the diverse technological processes used by different AKER-owned shipyards, have required doubling the number of AYDU employees. Additionally, the quality of the workforce needed to be enhanced through reskilling and upskilling not only skilled engineers but also university graduates, nearly the only source of new employees. The above circumstances presented a considerable challenge and were powerful drivers for Ukrainian shipbuilding education. An inherited version of the SDEU model for internal apprenticeship required significant enhancement and scaling of all curricula, including those for a broader range of shipbuilding specializations, other digital solutions, and software packages.

By 2009, the modified strategy had increased engineering staff by nearly 50%, and AYDU's share of exports had reached more than 95%. The company became a preferable outsourcer for the most effective shipyards of AKER Shipyards Group, utilizing the most innovative technologies, including some AI instruments. The quality and efficiency of the projects were still preserved on the highest European level. It was the next success story of a growing but resilient team. On the other hand, all SDEU export projects were contracted exclusively by Damen Group shipyards worldwide. The Group management decided to replicate the SDEU development success story to continue benefiting from the high quality and efficiency of engineering provided by the Ukrainian office.

MDEM (Marine Design Engineering Mykolaiv) was established in 2006 when the Spanish company ATN contracted a small group of engineers to design a seismic research vessel. The new Damen-owned office grew quickly, with stable loading from the group companies. Nowadays, MDEM consists of more than 200 employees, and among them are many NUOS graduates. Engineering services still form the core business of MDEM work and expertise. In addition, the MDEM portfolio has expanded with research and development, electrical and automation, engineering standards and part catalogue, online marketing, digital platforms support, and IT & IM GLOBAL. Furthermore, MDEM International became a widely known multiservice engineering company and MDEM management developed own original IRUM. Keeping its core business as the basic and detailed engineering for shipbuilding projects, it created additional digital services for Damen Shipyards Group and expanded its engineering services portfolio, meeting Damen standards on quality, time, and costs. Their contribution to educational programs at the NUOS extended beyond simply participating in developing a modern ship engineering training model. They also played a key role in establishing and enforcing the Chair of Intellectual Economy of the Sea, which focuses on digitalization using AI tools.

3.3.2 International academia-business collaboration in navigating Shipbuilding 4.0

An international collaboration between Ukrainian shipyards, design, and engineering offices started in 2009 when the global economic crisis affected shipowners' contracting of new ships. This led to a sharp reduction in financial flows and increased interest rates for banks' lending to shipbuilding. The former necessity for ongoing personnel replenishment during the global crisis was converted into a forced partial reduction in production resources. In response to these circumstances, AYDU and MDEM decided to transfer the knowledge and expertise related to the IRUM model to the NUOS. This transfer included methodological materials, training programs, databases of specialized training processes, and more. They were joined by Advanced Measuring Instruments Company LLC (AMICO), which was then Schneider Electric's systems integrator in Ukrainian maritime technology. Together, they committed to fulfilling the essential technological needs of the university's technological centers by providing computer equipment, application servers, Internet communications, and more. Moreover, taking advantage of their long-term and sustainable cooperation with the world market leaders in digital solutions for shipbuilding, they involved AVEVA, CADMATIC, and Schneider Electric in a newborn collaboration with NUOS teachers to provide efficient lifelong education (LLE) in Ukrainian shipbuilding.

The win-win cooperation (2009-2024). The NUOS established a new structural unit called the Research Institute of Contemporary Ship Engineering (INKI) [8]. All project stakeholders signed a multilateral cooperation agreement, and several bilateral agreements were to provide the necessary licensing packages. This began the next phase of developing a new shipbuilding education model. The model should focus on the dual transition requirements and competencies of the most current ship engineering specializations within the actual supply and value chains while gradually integrating AI tools. As a result of this development and cooperation, over a hundred INKI graduates (Figure 3.2) joined the national and international shipbuilding

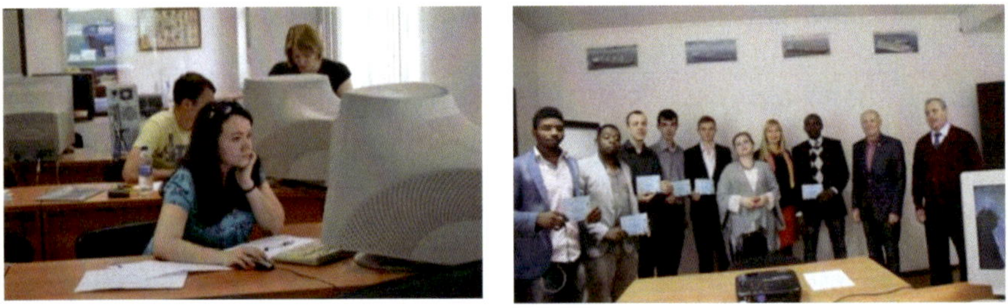

(a) (b)

Figure 3.2 Implementation of the laboratory workshop (a) and certificates conferment to graduates of the international group (b).

workforce, securing positions in the Ukrainian shipbuilding industry and abroad, including in countries such as the Netherlands, France, Norway, Finland, and Poland.

Outline of the competencies of the specializations within ship engineering. When considering the different specializations (Table 3.2) within

Table 3.2 AYDU engineers' competencies and educational emphasis

Engineer role	Unique competencies and emphasis	Challenges
Naval architect	Hydrodynamics, dynamics and stability, structural design, design software proficiency, etc. Curricula should emphasise physics, applied mathematics, and materials science, integrated with advanced design, engineering, job preparation, and simulation tools that reflect current maritime practices.	Additional CAD and SW systems, diversity of customers and new technology at their shipyards (new types of equipment, robots, etc.)
Mechanical engineer	Thermal systems design, dynamics and stability, energy efficiency technologies, maintenance and reliability engineering, etc. Mechanical engineering education should include hands-on training with machinery, thermodynamics, fluid mechanics, and advanced engineering principles relevant to marine environments.	Dynamic nomenclature changes of on-board machinery and marine fuels based on the dual transformation acceleration, etc.
Electrical engineer	Electrical distribution systems design, alternative energy sources, control systems, safety standards and regulations, integration of electrical and mechanical systems, etc. Electrical engineering programs should focus on power electronics, control theory, programming for automation, and signal processing, as well as practical workshops related to shipboard systems.	Introduction of green and autonomous ships demanding more complicated automation and navigation control systems utilizing diversified AI instruments.
Project managers	Project lifecycle management, budgeting and resource allocation, risk management; clients, engineers, and regulatory bodies communication. Project management education should include additional training in project management software (MS Project, Primavera, etc.) and practical business and leadership skills tailored to the maritime industry.	Capability to focus on integrating technical and managerial skills in the everyday work. MBA is preferred.
General projects managers	Team dynamics and leadership, technical oversight, time management and performance evaluation. Training for task team leaders should encompass contemporary technical knowledge relevant to their specialization team's tasks and soft skills essential for managing team dynamics, effective communication, and leadership.	Capability to manage multiple projects with different customers, optimizing the task team personnel distribution to projects. MBA is in place.

ship engineering, such as naval architects, mechanical engineers, electrical engineers, project managers, and task team leaders, it's essential to tailor educational and training focuses to address each role's unique competencies and challenges. Each ship engineering specialization requires a distinct focus on education and training to ensure that professionals are well-prepared for their roles in the shipbuilding and maritime industry.

Modified shipbuilding education model. The development of the shipbuilding education model within the network of international and cross-industrial cooperation was based on the "end-to-end" (E2E) idea of education and professional training. This refers to a comprehensive approach encompassing the entire learning and development process, from initial engagement with learners to their successful transition into the workforce. The jointly developed "Knowledge-skills-expertise-reskilling-upskilling" (KSERU) model assures learners that they are equipped with (a) theoretical knowledge [65], (b) practical skills [66–69], and (c) the support they need to thrive in their careers [2, 67]. It emphasizes collaboration between educational institutions, employers, and learners to create a seamless learning experience (Figure 3.3).

3.3.3 Discussion of AI tools application and future development

AI-driven predictive updates for internships, reskilling and upskilling curricula, and extracurricular activities, paired with the early development of a student's digital twin and continuous support throughout their professional

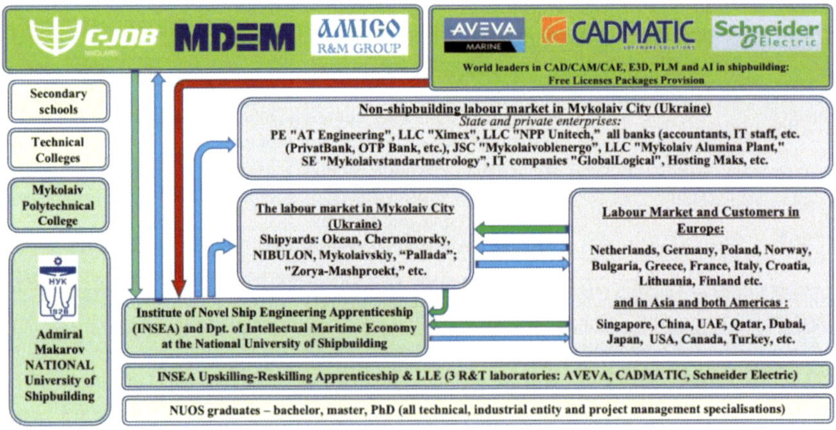

Figure 3.3 Ship Engineering 4.0 supply chain based on the KSERU model.

lives, can significantly enhance the timely growth of engineering expertise in shipbuilding [1, 2, 66]. However, the effectiveness of these initiatives largely relies on the commitment of faculty and students to embrace these technologies as early as possible. In this regard, polytechnic colleges should be vital; they were integrated into the relevant knowledge value chain with appropriately aligned curricula. Below are examples of successful AI tools used in the updated Institute of Novel Ship Engineering Apprenticeship (INSEA) concept. Vital aspects include AI modules embedded in the licensed software's digital solutions and innovative, jointly in-house-developed AI modules for KSERU.

AVEVA Marine P&ID Integrator Compare Tool. This module compares process and instrumentation diagrams (P&IDs) in the marine and offshore industries. It enables users to identify differences between two versions of P&IDs, which is essential for maintaining the accuracy of design documents and ensuring all stakeholders are informed of changes. Key features of the AVEVA Marine P&ID Integrator Compare tool typically include screens like those presented in Figure 3.4 and features shown in Table 3.3.

In addition to its advantages in visual management and control, the integrator compare tool provides an extensive dataset for a personal quantitative assessment of students' efficiency in laboratory work. This dataset includes information about the following time intervals connected to student S $(s = 1 \div M)$ (Figure 3.5) and derivative time intervals, namely: T_{fis} – the planned time to execute the laboratory task $i = 1 \div N;$ T_{iis} – self-checking time; T_{ris} – time spent on resolving issues after self-control; T_{eis} – time spent on

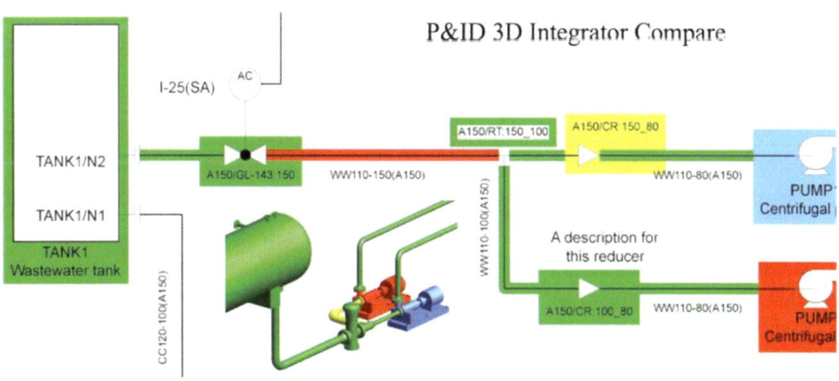

Figure 3.4 Example screen of AVEVA Marine P&ID Integrator Compare Tool (visuals legend: *green* – no inconsistencies, *yellow* – warning, *red* – error, *blue* – unresolved).

Table 3.3 Key Features of the AVEVA Marine P&ID Integrator Compare Tool

Key feature	**Tool designation and importance**
Visual comparison	Provides a graphical interface to visualize differences between two P&ID diagrams, making it easier to spot changes
Change detection	The tool highlights additions, deletions, and helps manage different versions of P&IDs, ensuring that updates are tracked and documented correctly
Version control	Helps manage different versions of P&IDs, ensuring that updates are tracked and documented correctly
Reporting	Generates reports summarizing the differences identified during the comparison, which can be helpful for audits and reviews
Integration with other tools	It often integrates seamlessly with other AVEVA Marine design tools, facilitating a smoother workflow in design and documentation processes. This comparison feature is essential for maintaining consistency and compliance in complex marine projects where changes can significantly affect safety and performance

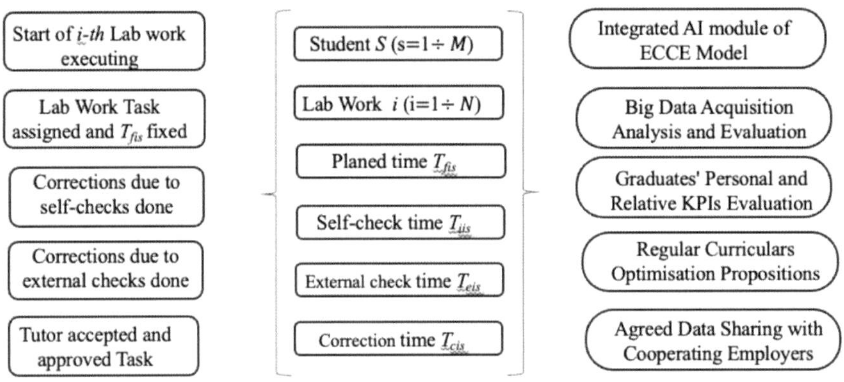

Figure 3.5 Scheme of the ECCE (executed, checked, corrected, evaluated) AI module.

resolving issues after external control; T_{cis} – overall correcting time; T_{LD} – total actual time of execution of accepted practical laboratory work $d = 1 \div D$, *etc.*

At the end of each laboratory session, an AI module is used. This module analyzes statistical data from MS Project (or similar project management platforms) and combines it with archived models and drawings from each laboratory work. It intelligently evaluates the completed tasks, calculates individual key performance indicators (KPIs), and contributes to the machine-learning process of each student's digital twin.

In the future, the system will use cloud analytics tools to provide recommendations for enhancing training programs. It will also suggest personalized tasks for return on experience (ROE) and offer relative ratings for each student compared to their group's average performance indicators and those of practicing engineers from various companies. Consequent data analysis is used to adjust the educational process and assess the student's progress in training and the competencies they have gained over time. This data may be shared with collaborating employers (if graduates agree).

3.4 Conclusion

This chapter discusses in detail the significant role of AI tools in increasing the efficiency of research, learning, and teaching processes in Ukraine's education system. The analysis includes the current state of digital transformation and AI implementation at Ukrainian universities, successful cases and challenges, and the role and perspective of AI application in the Ukrainian education system for accelerating Ukraine's post-war recovery.

The advances of Ukrainian universities (a) in AI introducing to educational processes, (b) in the practical efficiency of academic-industry collaborations, and (c) in creating innovative educational ecosystems, virtual education environments, and new laboratories on ML and robotics are reflected in the chapter based on the experience of the National Technical University of Ukraine "Igor Sikorsky Kyiv Polytechnic Institute," the Taras Shevchenko National University of Kyiv, National University "Lviv Polytechnic," Odesa National Academy of Food Technologies, National Technical University "Kharkiv Polytechnic University," the State University of Telecommunications, National Aviation University, Petro Mohyla Black Sea National University, and the Admiral Makarov National University of Shipbuilding. The results of successful cooperation with foreign universities are confirmed by joint teacher-student publications included in the database Scopus.

Special attention is paid to the digital transformation of shipbuilding education in Ukraine. Looking ahead, the role of AI in shipbuilding education and apprenticeships in Ukraine is expected to grow significantly. Collaboration between educational institutions and shipbuilding companies can improve curricula, ensuring they remain relevant to technological advancements. Additionally, government policies supporting AI integration into vocational training will be crucial for developing a skilled workforce capable of meeting the demands of a digitalized shipbuilding industry. In summary, thoughtfully integrating AI into Ukrainian shipbuilding education and apprenticeship programs offers unique opportunities to improve learning experiences, align educational outcomes with industry needs, and contribute to a revitalized shipbuilding sector. By addressing current challenges and fostering a culture of innovation, Ukraine can position itself as a strong partner in the international shipbuilding value chain in the age of AI, provided that appropriate investments are made.

Further research must be directed to gathering and summarizing the knowledge on AI development and implementation for strengthening academic-industry cooperation and spreading international experience between Ukrainian teachers, students, researchers, and developers with the goals of (a) additional motivation in AI implementation, (b) generation of new ideas into harnessing the power of LLMs for educational purposes, and (c) accelerating steps and increasing the efficiency of the activities on the AI and Ukrainian education system integration.

References

[1] Y. Kondratenko, et al. 'Tendencies and Challenges of Artificial Intelligence Development and Implementation,' in: IDAACS'2023 Proceedings, Vol. 1, 2023, pp. 221-226. DOI:10.1109/IDAACS58523.2023.10348800

[2] Y. Kondratenko, et al., 'Analysis of the Priorities and Perspectives in Artificial Intelligence Implementation,' 2023 13th International Conference on Dependable Systems, Services and Technologies, DESSERT 2023, 2023, Athens, 13 – 15 October 2023, DOI10.1109/DESSERT61349.2023.10416432

[3] A.I. Shevchenko, et al., 'Analysis of the prospect domains in AI implementation: Nationals, NATO and Ukraine AI strategies,' in: Y.P. Kondratenko, A.I. Shevchenko, (Eds). Research Tendencies and Prospect Domains for AI Development and Implementation, River Publishers, 2024, 1-30. https://www.riverpublishers.com/book_details.php?book_id=1163

[4] Y.P. Kondratenko, V.I. Slyusar, M.B. Solesvik, N.Y. Kondratenko, Z. Gomolka, 'Interrelation and inter-influence of artificial intelligence and higher education systems,' in: Y. Kondratenko, et al. (Eds) Research Tendencies and Prospect Domains for AI Development and Implementation, 2024, pp. 31–58. https://www.scopus.com/record/display.uri?eid=2-s2.0-85202992102&origin=resultslist

[5] V. Slyusar, et al., 'Some Aspects of Artificial Intelligence Development Strategy for Mobile Technologies,' Journal of Mobile Multimedia, Vol. 20, Iss. 03, 2024, pp. 525–554. https://doi.org/10.13052/jmm1550-4646.2031

[6] Y. Kondratenko, D. Simon, I. Atamanyuk, 'University Curricula Modification Based on Advancements in Information and Communication Technologies,' CEUR Workshop Proceedings, Vol. 1614, 2016, pp. 184–199. https://ceur-ws.org/Vol-1614/paper_18.pdf

[7] Y. Kondratenko, et al., 'Towards Implementing the Strategy of Artificial Intelligence Development: Ukraine Peculiarities,' CEUR Workshop Proceedings, Vol. 3513, 2023, pp. 106–117. https://ceur-ws.org/Vol-3513/paper09.pdf

[8] Yu.D. Zhukov, et al., 'The Use of Multimedia Teaching Aids in Teaching the Basics of Ship Engineering, Innovations in Shipbuilding & Maritime Infrastructure, No. 1(8), pp. 32-45, 2015.

[9] I. Tamozhska, et al., 'Innovative teaching methods for developing basic skills in higher education students through real professional contexts,' Salud, Ciencia y Tecnología – Serie de Conferencias 3, 2024, pp. 1-9. DOI:10.56294/sctconf2024.1214

[10] V. Honcharuk, et al., 'Educational Innovation and Digital Transformation: Interconnection and Prospects for Ukraine,' Futurity Education, 4(2) , 2024, pp. 61-85. https://doi.org/10.57125/FED.2024.06.25.04

[11] V.I. Bobrytska, et al., 'Artificial intelligence (AI) in Ukrainian Higher Education: A Comprehensive Study of Stakeholder Attitudes, Expectations and Concerns,' International Journal of Learning, Teaching and Educational Research, Vol. 23, No. 1, pp. 400-426, January 2024. https://doi.org/10.26803/ijlter.23.1.20

[12] M. Tetyana, Y. Kondratenko, I. Sidenko, G. Kondratenko, 'Computer Vision Mobile System for Education Using Augmented Reality Technology,' Journal of Mobile Multimedia, Vol. 17, Is. 4, 2021, pp. 555-576. DOI:10.13052/jmm1550-4646.1744

[13] V. Shebanin, et al., 'Development of the Mathematical Model of the Informational Resource of a Distance Learning System', in: O. Chertov, et al. (eds.), Recent Developments in Data Science and Intelligent Analysis of Information, ICDSIAI 2018 Proceedings, Advances in Intelligent Systems and Computing, Vol. 836, Springer, Cham, 2019, pp. 199-205. DOI:10.1007/978-3-319-97885-7_20

[14] O. Kudria, et al., 'The Role of Innovative Techniques in Development of STEM education in Ukraine,' Academia, Number 35-36, 2024. http://hepnet.upatras.gr

[15] V. Kosenko, et al., 'Challenges and prospects for the development of online education in Ukraine: implementation experience and ways of further development,' Conhecimento & Diversidade, Niterói, Vol. 16, No. 43, Jul./Sept. 2024, pp. 192-209.
[16] M. Hnatyuk, et al., 'Implementing smart technologies for teaching Ukrainian language across secondary and higher education: Case studies and practical recommendations,' Multidisciplinary Science Journal, 2024, 6:e2024ss0716, pp. 1-8. https://doi.org/10.31893/multiscience.2024ss0716
[17] T. Kovaliuk, N. Kobets, 'The Concept of an Innovative Educational Ecosystem of Ukraine in the Context of the Approach "Education 4.0 for Industry 4.0",' CEUR Workshop Proceedings, Vol. 3013, 2021, pp. 106-120. https://ceur-ws.org/Vol-3013/20210106.pdf
[18] 'Educational programs in the field of artificial intelligence,' Ministry for Digital Transformation of Ukraine, 2021. URL: https://thedigital.gov.ua/lms_ai
[19] S. Vasylyuk-Zaitseva, et al., 'Application of Artificial Intelligence in Ukrainian Education of the Future,' Futurity Education, Vol. 3(3), 2023, pp. 79–107.
[20] D.A. Pokryshen, 'Evaluation of satisfaction with the use of artificial intelligence in the educational process by teachers in Ukraine,' CEUR Workshop Proceedings, Vol. 3781, 2024, pp. 132-144. https://ceur-ws.org/Vol-3781/paper16.pdf
[21] 'Tech Ecosystem Guide to Ukraine,' 2019. URL: https://data.unit.city/tech-guide/Tech_Ecosystem_Guide_To_Ukraine_En-1.1.pdf
[22] Sikorsky Challenge innovation ecosystem. URL: https://kpi.ua/ru/ecoino
[23] SoftServe University. URL: https://www.softserveinc.com/uk-ua/university
[24] I. Atamanyuk, et al., 'Computer's Analysis Method and Reliability Assessment of Fault-Tolerance Operation of Information Systems,' CEUR Workshop Proceedings, Vol. 1356, pp. 507-522, 2015. https://ceur-ws.org/Vol-1356/paper_52.pdf
[25] A. Sheremet, et al., 'Diagnosis of Lung Disease Based on Medical Images Using Artificial Neural Networks,' IEEE 3rd Ukraine Conf. on Electrical and Computer Engineering (UKRCON), 2021, 561–566. DOI:10.1109/UKRCON53503.2021.9575961

[26] I. Sova, et al., 'Machine learning technology for neoplasm segmentation on brain MRI scans,' CEUR Workshop Proceedings, Vol. 2791, 2020, pp. 50–59. https://ceur-ws.org/Vol-2791/2020200050.pdf

[27] Y. Kondratenko, I. Sidenko, G. Kondratenko, V. Petrovych, M. Taranov, I. Sova, 'Artificial Neural Networks for Recognition of Brain Tumors on MRI Images,' in: A. Bollin et al. (eds) Information and Communication Technologies in Education, Research, and Industrial Applications, Communications in Computer and Information Science, Vol. 1308, Springer, Cham, 2021, pp. 119-140. DOI: https://doi.org/10.1007/978-3-030-77592-6_6

[28] Y.P. Kondratenko, J. Rudolph, O.V. Kozlov, Y.M. Zaporozhets, O.S. Gerasin, 'Neuro-fuzzy observers of clamping force for magnetically operated movers of mobile robots,' Technical Electrodynamics, No. 5, 2017, pp. 53-61. DOI:10.15407/techned2017.05.053

[29] A. Sokoliuk, et al., 'Machine Learning Algorithms for Binary Classification of Liver Disease,' in: 2020 IEEE Int. Conf. on Problems of Infocommunications, Science and Technology (PIC S&T), 2020, pp. 417-421. DOI:10.1109/PICST51311.2020.9468051.

[30] Y. Kondratenko, G. Khademi, V. Azimi, D. Ebeigbe, M. Abdelhady, S.A. Fakoorian, T. Barto, A.Y.Roshanineshat, I. Atamanyuk, D. Simon, 'Robotics and Prosthetics at Cleveland State University: Modern Information, Communication, and Modeling Technologies,' in: A. Ginige, et al. (Eds) Information and Communication Technologies in Education, Research, and Industrial Applications (ICTERI), Communications in Computer and Information Science, Vol. 783, Springer, Cham, 2017, pp. 133–155. https://doi.org/10.1007/978-3-319-69965-3_8

[31] Y. Kondratenko, G. Khademi, V. Azimi, D. Ebeigbe, M. Abdelhady, S.A. Fakoorian, T. Barto, A.Y.Roshanineshat, I. Atamanyuk, D. Simon, 'Information, Communication, and Modeling Technologies in Prosthetic Leg and Robotics Research at Cleveland State University,' CEUR Workshop Proceedings, Vol. 1614, 2016, pp. 168-183. http://ceur-ws.org/Vol-1614/paper_34.pdf

[32] R. Leizerovych, et al., 'IoT-complex for Monitoring and Analysis of Motor Highway Condition Using Artificial Neural Networks,' Proceedings - 2020 IEEE 11th Int. Conference on Dependable Systems, Services and Technologies (DESSERT), Kyiv, Ukraine, 2020, pp. 207-212. DOI: 10.1109/DESSERT50317.2020.9125004

[33] K. Ivanova, et al., 'Artificial intelligence in automated system for web-interfaces visual testing,' CEUR Workshop Proceedings, Vol. 2604, 2020, pp. 1019-1031. https://ceur-ws.org/Vol-2604/paper68.pdf
[34] I. Khortiuk, et al., 'Scoring system based on neural networks for identification of factors in image perception,' Vol. 2604, 2020, pp. 993-1003. https://ceur-ws.org/Vol-2604/paper66.pdf
[35] G. Kondratenko, et al., 'Mobile Recognition of Image Components Based on Machine Learning Methods,' Journal of Mobile Multimedia, Vol. 20, Issue 3, 2024, pp. 699–726. DOI:10.13052/jmm1550-4646.2038
[36] I. Sidenko, G. Kondratenko, O. Heras, et al., 'Neural Technologies for Objects Classification with Mobile Applications,' Journal of Mobile Multimedia, Vol. 20, Issue 3, 2024, pp. 727–748. DOI:10.13052/jmm1550-4646.2039
[37] V. Timchenko, V. Kreinovich, Y. Kondratenko, V. Horbov, 'Hybrid Fuzzy-Color Computing Based on Optical Logical Architecture,' in: C. Kahraman, et al. (eds) Intelligent and Fuzzy Systems, INFUS 2024, Lecture Notes in Networks and Systems, Vol. 1090, Springer, Cham, 2024, pp. 266–274. https://doi.org/10.1007/978-3-031-67192-0_33
[38] Y.P. Kondratenko, N.Y. Kondratenko, 'Soft Computing Analytic Models for Increasing Efficiency of Fuzzy Information Processing in Decision Support Systems,' in: R. Hudson (Eds) Decision Making: Processes, Behavioral Influences and Role in Business Management, Nova Science Publ., New York, pp. 41-78, 2015. ISBN 978-163483013-3
[39] Y. Kondratenko, N. Kondratenko, 'Real-Time Fuzzy Data Processing Based on a Computational Library of Analytic Models,' Data, Volume 3, Issue 4, 59, 2018. doi:10.3390/data3040059.
[40] Y. Kondratenko, N. Kondratenko, 'Reduced library of the soft computing analytic models for arithmetic operations with asymmetrical fuzzy numbers,' in: Alan Casey (Ed) Soft Computing: Developments, Methods and Applications, NOVA Science Publishers, Hauppauge, New York, 2016, pp. 1-38. ISBN 978-163485151-0
[41] Y. Kondratenko, N. Kondratenko, 'Soft Computing Analytic Models for Multiplication of Asymmetrical Fuzzy Numbers,' in: S.N. Shahbazova, et al. (eds) Recent Developments and the New Direction in Soft-Computing Foundations and Applications, Studies in Fuzziness and Soft Computing, Vol. 393, Springer, Cham, 2021, pp. 201-214. DOI:10.1007/978-3-030-47124-8_17

[42] Y. Kondratenko, N. Kondratenko, 'Computational Library of the Direct Analytic Models for Real-Time Fuzzy Information Processing,' Proc. 2018 IEEE Second Int. Conf. on Data Stream Mining & Processing (DSMP), Lviv, Ukraine, 21–25 August 2018, pp. 38–43. DOI:10.110 9/DSMP.2018.8478518

[43] Y. Kondratenko, N. Kondratenko, 'Universal direct analytic models for the minimum of triangular fuzzy numbers,' In: CEUR Workshop Proceedings, Vol. 2104, 2018, pp. 100-115. https://ceur-ws.org/Vol-21 04/paper_208.pdf

[44] Y.P. Kondratenko, N.Y. Kondratenko, 'Synthesis of Analytic Models for Subtraction of Fuzzy Numbers with Various Membership Function's Shapes,' in: A. Gil-Lafuente, et al. (eds) Applied Mathematics and Computational Intelligence, FIM 2015, Advances in Intelligent Systems and Computing, Vol. 730. Springer, Cham, pp. 87-100, 2018. https: //doi.org/10.1007/978-3-319-75792-6_8

[45] Y. Kondratenko, S. Sichevskyi, et al., 'Manipulator's Control System with Application of the Machine Learning,' 11th IEEE Intern. Conf. on Intelligent Data Acquisition and Advanced Computing Systems: Technology and Applications (IDAACS), Cracow, Poland, pp. 363-368, 2021. DOI:10.1109/IDAACS53288.2021.9660910

[46] Y. Kondratenko, I. Atamanyuk, I. Sidenko, G. Kondratenko, S. Sichevskyi, 'Machine Learning Techniques for Increasing Efficiency of the Robot's Sensor and Control Information Processing,' Sensors, Vol. 22, 2022, 1062. https://doi.org/10.3390/s22031062

[47] A.M. Topalov, et al., 'Computerized intelligent system for remote diagnostics of level sensors in the floating dock ballast complexes,' CEUR Workshop Proceedings, Vol. 2105, 2018, pp. 94-108. https://ceur-ws.or g/Vol-2105/10000094.pdf

[48] O. Chornovol, et al., 'Intelligent forecasting system for NPP's energy production,' Proceedings of the 2020 IEEE 3rd International Conference on Data Stream Mining and Processing (DSMP), Lviv, 2020, pp. 102-107. DOI:10.1109/DSMP47368.2020.9204275

[49] M. Taranov, C. Wolf, J. Rudolph, et al., 'Simulation of Robot's Wheel-Mover on Ferromagnetic Surfaces,' Proc. 2017 IEEE 9th Int. Conf. IDAACS, Vol. 1, Bucharest, Romania, Sept. 21-23, 2017, pp. 283-288. DOI: 10.1109/IDAACS.2017.8095091

[50] O. Kovaliv, et al., 'Neural Network Architectures for Recognizing Military Objects on Satellite Images,' 12th IEEE Intern. Conf. on Intelligent

Data Acquisition and Advanced Computing Systems: Technology and Applications (IDAACS), Dortmund, 2023, pp. 175-180. DOI:10.1109/IDAACS58523.2023.10348905

[51] O. Kozlov, et al., 'Intelligent IoT-based Control System of the UAV for Meteorological Measurements,' Journal of Mobile Multimedia, 2024, Vol. 20, Issue 3, pp. 555–596. DOI:10.13052/jmm1550-4646.2032

[52] O.V. Kozlov, et al., 'Information Technology for Parametric Optimization of Fuzzy Systems Based on Hybrid Grey Wolf Algorithms,' SN Computer Science, 3(6), 463, 2022. DOI: 10.1007/s42979-022-01333-4

[53] O. Skakodub, et al., 'Optimization of Linguistic Terms' Shapes and Parameters: Fuzzy Control System of a Quadrotor Drone. Proc. IDAACS 2021, Vol. 1, pp. 566–571, 2021, Cracow, Poland, 22-25 September 2021, 176232. DOI:10.1109/IDAACS53288.2021.9660926

[54] O. Striuk, et al., 'Generative adversarial neural network for creating photorealistic images,' 2020 IEEE 2nd Intern. Conf. on Advanced Trends in Information Theory (ATIT), Kyiv, Ukraine, 2020, pp. 368-371. DOI: 10.1109/ATIT50783.2020.9349326

[55] O. Striuk, et al., 'Adaptive Deep Convolutional GAN for Fingerprint Sample Synthesis,' 2021 IEEE 4th Intern. Conf. on Advanced Information and Communication Technologies (AICT), Lviv, 2021, pp. 193-196. DOI:10.1109/AICT52120.2021.9628978

[56] Taranov, M., Rudolph, J., Wolf, C., Kondratenko, Y., Gerasin, O. 'Advanced approaches to reduce number of actors in a magnetically-operated wheel-mover of a mobile robot,' 2017 13th Int. Conf. Perspective Technologies and Methods in MEMS Design, (MEMSTECH), Proceedings, 2017. pp. 96-100. DOI:10.1109/MEMSTECH.2017.7937542

[57] D. Hapishko, et al., 'Modification of Fuzzy TOPSIS Based on Various Proximity Coefficients Metrics and Shapes of Fuzzy Sets,' in: G. Antoniou, G., et al. Information and Communication Technologies in Education, Research, and Industrial Applications (ICTERI), Communications in Computer and Information Science, Vol. 1980, Springer, Cham, 2023, pp. 98–113. https://doi.org/10.1007/978-3-031-48325-7_8

[58] Y. Kondratenko, O. Gerasin, A. Topalov, 'A simulation model for robot's slip displacement sensors,' International Journal of Computing, Vol. 15, Issue 4, Open Access, 2016, pp. 224-236. http://www.computingonline.net/computing/article/viewFile/854/768

[59] I. Sidenko, A. Trukhov, G. Kondratenko, Y. Zhukov, Y. Kondratenko, 'Machine Learning for Unmanned Aerial Vehicle Routing on Rough Terrain,' in: Z. Hu, et al. (eds) Advances in Computer Science for Engineering and Education VI (ICCSEEA), Lecture Notes on Data Engineering and Communications Technologies, Vol. 181, Springer, Cham, 2023, pp. 626–635. DOI:10.1007/978-3-031-36118-0_56

[60] I. Sidenko, K. Filina, G. Kondratenko, D. Chabanovskyi, Y. Kondratenko, 'Eye-tracking technology for the analysis of dynamic data,' 2018 IEEE 9th International Conference on Dependable Systems, Services and Technologies, (DESSERT), Kyiv, Ukraine, 2018, pp. 509-514. DOI:10.1109/DESSERT.2018.8409181

[61] Y. Kondratenko, E. Gordienko, 'Implementation of the neural networks for adaptive control system on FPGA,' B. Katalinic (Ed.), Annals DAAAM & Proc. 23th Int. DAAAM Symp. "Intelligent Manufacturing and Automation", Vol. 23, No. 1, Vienna, Austria, EU, 2012, pp. 0389-0392. DOI:10.2507/23rd.daaam.proceedings.090

[62] R. Semeniuk, et al., 'Innovative Methodologies and Approaches to Teaching with Artificial Intelligence in Ukrainian Higher Education,' Futurity Education, Vol. 4(1), 2024, pp. 24-52. https://doi.org/10.57125/FED.2024.03.25.02

[63] S. Dillon, B. Clark, 'Learning during Crisis: Insights for Ukraine from across the Globe,' OECD Publishing, 2024, pp. 1-45.

[64] V.D. Zalizko, et al., 'Assessing Ukrainian education security in the context of artificial intelligence integration for accelerated post-war recovery," Scientific Bulletin of National Mining University, Vol. 6, 2024, pp. 119-128. DOI:10.33271/nvngu/2024-6/119

[65] R. Dokkum, 'Ship knowledge: ship design construction and operation,' Dokmar Maritime Publishers, 11th edition, 2024.

[66] Yu. Zhukov, et al., 'The Current State and Prospects of the Use of the Distance Learning Instruments During Study of Ship Engineering,' Information Technologies and Learning Tools, Vol. 87, Iss. 1, 2022, pp. 151–165. https://doi.org/10.33407/itlt.v87i1.4505

[67] Y. Zhukov, O. Zivenko, 'Ship Operation Analysis and Optimization via Mobile Application,' Journal of Mobile Multimedia, Vol. 20, Iss. 3, 2024, pp. 627-650. DOI:https://doi.org/10.13052/jmm1550-4646.2034

[68] Y. Kondratenko, S. Sidorenko, 'Ship Navigation in Narrowness Passes and Channels in Uncertain Conditions: Intelligent Decision Support,'

in: P. Shi, et al. (eds) Complex Systems: Spanning Control and Computational Cybernetics: Foundations, Studies in Systems, Decision and Control, Vol. 414, Springer, Cham, 475–493, 2022. DOI:10.1007/978-3-030-99776-2_24

[69] Y.P. Kondratenko, G.F. Romanovsky, D.M. Pidopryhora, G.V. Kondratenko, 'Optimal planning of cargo operations at bunkering tankers with respect to dynamical character of their parameter restrictions,' IFAC Proceedings Volumes, Vol. 37, Issue 10, pp. 239–244, 2004. ISSN 1474-6670. https://doi.org/10.1016/S1474-6670(17)31738-X

4

Best Strategies for Bilingual Education: How Can We Explain Their Success?

Claudia Cabrera[1], Olga Kosheleva[1], Christian Servin[2], and Vladik Kreinovich[3]

[1]Department of Teacher Education
University of Texas at El Paso, USA
[2]Information Technology Systems Department
El Paso Community College (EPCC), USA
[3]Department of Computer Science
University of Texas at El Paso, USA
E-mail: olgak@utep.edu; cservin1@epcc.edu; vladik@utep.edu

Abstract

When designing AI-based tools for education, it is important to take into account the experience of human teachers. In this, it is necessary to distinguish between the education features that are justified by the general features of the corresponding education task – these features should be taken into account in AI-based learning as well – and features which are specific for traditional non-AI teaching. In this chapter, on the important example of bilingual education, we show that several empirically successful teaching strategies can be explained in the general context – and thus, should be implemented in AI-based teaching as well.

4.1 Introduction

Bilingual education is important. In the border area between domains of speakers of different languages, many people are bilingual. To function well in such an environment, it is important to train the students to be able to perform well in both languages. This is the main objective of bilingual education.

DOI: 10.1201/9788743809258-4

As with other education needs (see, e.g., [4]), it is desirable to use all education tools – including AI tools (see, e.g., [2]) – to help. In designing such a help, it is natural to take into account the experience of traditional – non-AI – bilingual education. To better utilize this experience, it is important to understand which bilingual education strategies are justified by the general features of the corresponding learning tasks – features not depending on:

- whether teaching is done by human teacher only
- or by an AI-based education system.

These features need to be implemented in the AI-based system as well – while it does not necessarily make sense to implement strategies which are specific for human teachers.

From this viewpoint, it is important to analyze the existing strategies for bilingual education – which of them have deep justifications and which are specific for human teachers.

What we do in this chapter. Our paper is based on the dissertation [1] that describes, in detail, the semi-empirically determined setting of a successful bilingual education program. In this chapter, we provide a general theoretical explanation for the success of these particular settings.

The structure of the chapter. In this section, we describe the general successful settings. In the following sections, for each of these settings, we provide a theoretical explanation.

What are the settings that we plan to explain. The first two settings relate to pre-planning of the overall teaching process.

- First, in the successful program, 50% of the time the material is taught in English, with some connections to Spanish, and 50% of the material is taught in Spanish, with some connections to English. This is different of many other bilingual programs where the proportion of languages is 80/20 or 90/10 [3].
- Second, in this program, each day, half of the day is in one language, half is in another language, with the order of the languages changing from each day to the next.
- The third setting is related to the actual teaching process: it is important *not* to correct minor mistakes all the time.

Finally, the fourth and the fifth settings are related to the assessment of students' leearning:

- The fourth setting is that it is important to regularly show, to students, their progress.
- The fifth setting is that it is important to grade the students you know – and if several instructors participate in grading, the grades by instructors who know the students should have more weights in the resulting grade.

4.2 Why 50/50 Distribution Between Languages

Mathematical model. In this section, we provide a possible explanation of why 50/50 distribution between languages works the best. This explanation is based on the following idea.

In general, teaching any topic requires several repetitions. On each repeti tion i, the student's understanding is not perfect: some ideas are remembered, but, in general, the knowledge is different from ideal. In other words, there is a difference $\Delta u_i \stackrel{\text{def}}{=} \widetilde{u}_i - u$ between the student's understanding $\widetilde{u}_i$ of the material presented on this iteration and the ideal perfect understanding u. Based on several understandings $\widetilde{u}_1, \ldots, \widetilde{u}_n$ of the presented material, the student forms the resulting picture $\widetilde{u}$. In this formation, the student naturally wants to select $\widetilde{u}$ which is close to all previous understandings, i.e., for which the resulting vector $(\widetilde{u}, \ldots, \widetilde{u})$ is as close as possible to the perceived vector $(\widetilde{u}_1, \ldots, \widetilde{u}_n)$. By Pythagoras theorem, the square d^2 of the distance d between the two vectors is equal to the sum of the squares of the differences between the values:

$$d^2 = (\widetilde{u} - \widetilde{u}_1)^2 + \ldots + (\widetilde{u} - \widetilde{u}_n)^2. \tag{4.1}$$

Minimizing the distance d is, of course, equivalent to minimizing its square d^2. We can minimize the expression eqn (4.1) if we simply use one of the main ideas from calculus: that in the location where the minimum is attained, the derivative of the objective function is equal to 0. Differentiating the expression eqn (4.1) with respect to the unknown $\widetilde{u}$ and equating the derivative to 0, we conclude that

$$2(\widetilde{u} - \widetilde{u}_1) + \ldots + 2(\widetilde{u} - \widetilde{u}_n) = 0. \tag{4.2}$$

Moving all the terms $\widetilde{u}_i$ to the right-hand side and dividing both sides by $2n$, we conclude that:

$$\widetilde{u} = \frac{\widetilde{u}_1 + \ldots + \widetilde{u}_n}{n}.$$

The resulting inaccuracy $\Delta u \stackrel{\text{def}}{=} \widetilde{u} - u$ of the student's understanding can be estimated if we subtract u from both sides of the eqn (4.2). Then, we get:

$$\Delta u = \frac{\Delta u_1 + \ldots + \Delta u_n}{n}. \tag{4.3}$$

Ideally, this difference should be as close to the ideal case 0 as possible. In other words, we want to make sure that the vector $(\Delta u^{(1)}, \ldots, \Delta u^{(K)})$ describing the understanding of all students is as close to the ideal vector $(0, \ldots, 0)$ as possible. Similarly to what we described above, this means minimizing the sum of the squares

$$\left(\Delta u^{(1)}\right)^2 + \ldots + \left(\Delta u^{(K)}\right)^2.$$

In mathematical terms, if we consider a population of students, this sum of the squares is proportional to the variance $\sigma^2 \stackrel{\text{def}}{=} E[(\Delta u)^2]$ of the value Δu. We therefore want to select a teaching strategy for which this variance is as small as possible.

In general, we have

$$\sigma^2 \stackrel{\text{def}}{=} E[(\Delta u)^2] = \frac{1}{n^2} \cdot E\left[\left(\sum_{i=1}^{n} \Delta u_i\right)^2\right] =$$

$$\frac{1}{n^2} \cdot \left(\sum_{i=1}^{n} E\left[(\Delta u_i)^2\right] + \sum_{i=1}^{n} \sum_{j \neq i} E\left[\Delta u_i \cdot \Delta u_j\right]\right). \tag{4.4}$$

Let us denote $E\left[(\Delta u_i)^2\right]$ by σ_i^2. Then, by definition of correlation r_{ij}, we have

$$E\left[(\Delta u_i)^2\right] = r_{ij} \cdot \sigma_i \cdot \sigma_j,$$

so the eqn (4.4) takes the following form:

$$\sigma^2 = \frac{1}{n^2} \cdot \left(\sum_{i=1}^{n} \sigma_i^2 + \sum_{i=1}^{n} \sum_{j \neq i} r_{ij} \cdot \sigma_i \cdot \sigma_j\right). \tag{4.5}$$

Mathematical model: analysis and the resulting explanation.

To estimate the variance σ^2, let us denote:

- the number of English lessons by n_E and
- the number of Spanish lessons by n_S.

Let us also denote:

- the average standard deviation of a single lesson by σ_0^2;
- the typical correlation between two lessons in the same language by r_s; and
- the typical correlation between two lessons in different languages by r_d.

Intuitively, since the two languages are different, correlation between lessons in different languages should be smaller than correlation between lessons in the same language: $r_d < r_s$.

In terms of σ_0, n_E, n_S, and correlations, the eqn (4.5) takes the following form:

$$\sigma^2 = \frac{\sigma_0^2}{n^2} \cdot \left(n + (n_E^2 - n_E) \cdot r_s + (n_S^2 - n_S) \cdot r_s + 2 \cdot n_E \cdot n_S \cdot r_d\right). \quad (4.6)$$

We want to explain why it is effective to use

$$n_E = n_S = \frac{n}{2}.$$

In other words, we want to explain why it is effective to have the difference

$$\delta \stackrel{\text{def}}{=} n_E - \frac{n}{2}$$

equal to 0. In terms of this difference, we have

$$n_E = \frac{n}{2} + \delta$$

and

$$n_S = n - n_E = n - \left(\frac{n}{2} + \delta\right) = \frac{n}{2} - \delta.$$

Substituting these expressions for n_E and n_S into the formula eqn (4.6), we get the following formula:

$$\sigma^2 = \frac{\sigma_0^2}{n^2} \cdot \left(n + r_s \cdot \left[\left(\frac{n}{2} + \delta\right)^2 - \left(\frac{n}{2} + \delta\right) + \left(\frac{n}{2} - \delta\right)^2 - \left(\frac{n}{2} - \delta\right)\right]\right.$$
$$\left. + 2r_d \cdot \left[\left(\frac{n}{2} + \delta\right) \cdot \left(\frac{n}{2} - \delta\right)\right]\right). \quad (4.7)$$

Here,

$$\left(\frac{n}{2}+\delta\right)^2-\left(\frac{n}{2}+\delta\right)+\left(\frac{n}{2}-\delta\right)^2-\left(\frac{n}{2}-\delta\right)$$
$$=\frac{n^2}{4}+n\cdot\delta+\delta^2-\frac{n}{2}-\delta+\frac{n^2}{4}-n\cdot\delta+\delta^2-\frac{n}{2}+\delta=\frac{n^2}{2}+2\delta^2-n,$$

and

$$2\cdot\left(\frac{n}{2}+\delta\right)\cdot\left(\frac{n}{2}-\delta\right)=2\cdot\left(\frac{n^2}{4}-\delta^2\right)=\frac{n^2}{2}-2\delta^2.$$

Thus, the formula eqn (4.7) takes the form

$$\sigma^2=\frac{\sigma_0^2}{n^2}\cdot\left(n+r_s\cdot\left(\frac{n^2}{2}+2\delta^2-n\right)+r_d\cdot\left(\frac{n^2}{2}-2\delta^2\right)\right)$$
$$=\frac{\sigma_0^2}{n^2}\cdot\left(n\cdot(1-r_s)+\frac{n^2}{2}\cdot(r_s+r_d)+2\delta^2\cdot(r_s-r_d)\right). \quad (4.8)$$

Since $r_s > r_d$, the eqn (4.8) is an increasing function of δ^2. Thus, its smallest value is attained when δ^2 is the smallest – i.e., when $\delta = 0$ and thus,

$$n_E = n_S = \frac{n}{2}.$$

This is exactly what we tried to explain.

4.3 Why Daily Switches Between Languages

Empirical fact. The 50/50 arrangement – that is, as we have shown, optimal – could be, in principle, arranged by studying in one of the languages one day, and in another language the next class day. However, it turned out that the more effective arrangement is when each day:

- first the teaching is in one of the languages; and
- then, in the second part of the school day, the teaching is in another language.

The language with which we start changes from one day to the next. For example:

- if the first half of Monday is in English;
- then the first half of Tuesday is in Spanish, etc.

Our explanation. Why? Here, the explanation is straightforward, does not require math. We want students:

- not only to learn the material;
- we also want them to be able to switch between languages on a short notice.

To teach this ability to the students, a natural idea is to train them on this transition every day. That is why it is useful to have language switches every day.

The same need explains the daily change the order of languages. Indeed:

- if we start with English every day;
- then students will learn how to switch from English to Spanish; but
- they will not become trained in fast switching from Spanish to English.

Students need to be trained to switch in both directions equally well – this is why we alternate the languages that start the school day.

4.4 Why It Is Important Not to Correct Minor Mistakes All the Time

Empirical fact. As students go through the process of acquiring new knowledge, their knowledge is not yet perfect, they make mistakes. At first glance, it seems reasonable to correct these mistakes – otherwise, how will the students know that they have made a mistake? In practice, however, the practice of always correcting all mistakes, major and minor, hinders education. It is much more effective *not* to correct mistakes all the time.

Mathematical model. In this section, we explain, on a simple mathematical model, why always correcting minor mistakes may be harmful. We will explain this phenomenon by using the following geometric representation of knowledge.

At any given moment of time, we can describe the state of a student's knowledge by a tuple $g = (g_1, g_2, \ldots)$ of relevant numbers – e.g., grades on different assignments. Each such tuple can be viewed as a point in the corresponding multi-D space, a point with coordinates g_1, g_2, etc. In these terms, the process of learning is described by a trajectory that leads the student:

- from their starting state S
- to as close as possible to the desired state D of perfect knowledge.

The ideal situation is when the student's trajectory brings them from the original state S to the desired state D by the fastest possible path. Let

F denote the first step on this ideal trajectory. In practice, students are not perfect. So:

- instead of reaching the desired intermediate state F;
- students reach a somewhat different state F'.

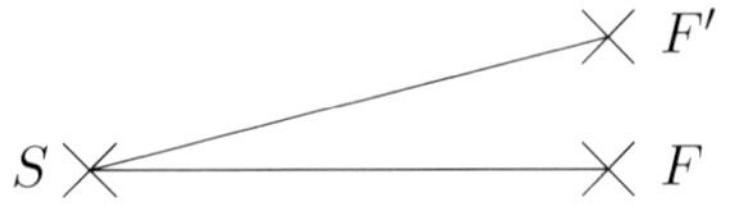

Resulting explanation. At first glance, in this situation, it makes sense to inform the student about their mistake. This way, the student will get to the correct intermediate state F – which will bring this student closer to the desired ideal state D.

However, the problem with this approach is that the student is not well aware of their location and direction: the reason why the student reached the state F' instead of the desired intermediate state F is that, at this stage of the student's knowledge, this student is not yet able to distinguish between F and F'. So:

- even if the student understands the direction in which the correction needs to be made – namely, the direction from F' to F;
- there is a good chance that result in an overcorrection, with the new state F'' possible event further from F than F'.

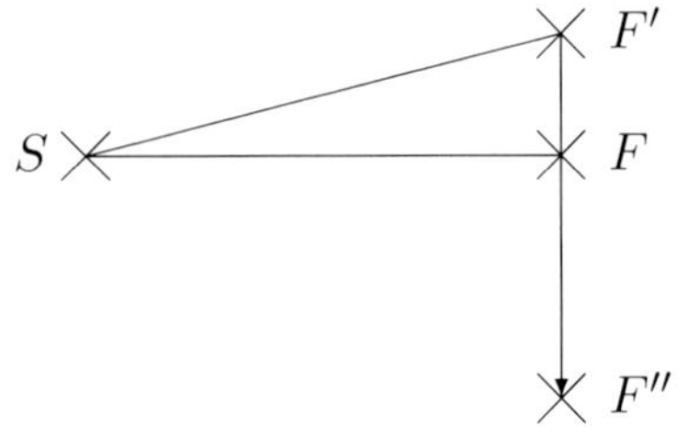

To avoid such an overcorrection, it is desirable to limit corrections only to *major* mistakes, mistakes for which the student is able – with a little help – to see the difference between the desired and the actual states.

4.5 Why It Is Important To Regularly Show, To Students, Their Progress

Our explanation: main idea. Even when students make progress that is clear to the instructor, students – as we have mentioned in the previous section – may not be skilled enough to detect small improvement in their knowledge. As a result, by comparing their state of knowledge before and after the class – or before and after their individual discussion with an instructor or with a teaching assistant – students may not see the difference and thus, get discouraged. One of us (VK) had this experience when taking Basic Spanish for Faculty class – when his grade after the first test turned out to be similar to his grade on a similar previous quiz.

To avoid such discouragements, it is desirable to explicitly remind the students of their state of knowledge at earlier stages of the class: this difference is much larger and is, thus, has a higher possibility to be visible to students.

Let us reformulate our explanation in terms of a simple mathematical model. Let us describe the above explanation in more mathematical terms. At the intermediate stage of their studies, student cannot tell the difference between their knowledge states $K(t')$ and $K(t)$ at two consequent moments of time $t' < t$ when the distance $d(K(t'), K(t))$ between these two states is smaller than some threshold $\varepsilon > 0$.

Students naturally compare their current knowledge state $K(t)$ with the most recent state – since this is the state that happened most recently and is, thus, best remembered. When t' is close to t, the state $K(t')$ is close to $K(t)$ – and thus, it is highly probable that the distance $d(K(t'), K(t))$ will be smaller than ε.

Thus, to make the progress visible, it is important to remind the students about their earlier knowledge states, at a moment $t'' \ll t'$ – this way the distance $d(K(t''), K(t))$ will be larger and thus, have more chances to be visible to students.

4.6 Why It Is Important To Grade Students You Know – And For Committee Grading, To Give More Weight To Grades Of Instructors Who Know The Student

Empirical fact. At first glance, it may seem that the most objective grading comes from outside graders: these graders will judge the level of knowledge shown on the test, without their opinion being prejudiced by the previous successes and failures of this particular student.

To some extent, this is correct. However, empirical data shows that for the most effective teaching, it is desirable to have grading done by instructors who know the student – and when the grading is done by a committee, grades by instructors who know the student should get more weight.

How we usually grade. To explain this empirical fact, let us recall that usually, the overall grade for a test is computed as an average – or a weighted average – of grades for individual problems, and the overall grade for a class is similarly computed as an average or as a weighted average of grades for all tests and graded assignments. Similarly to what we described earlier – when we talked about student's knowledge $\widetilde{u}$ after n classes, the average naturally appears if we are trying to find the overall grade that is the best fit for all the component grades.

Resulting explanation. However, the above argument does not take into account that once in a while, we have *outliers*: e.g., a student had a bad day and gets 0 on a test, not because of the lack of knowledge, but because of some stressful event unrelated to class.

Outliers occur in statistics in general: a measuring instrument can malfunction, etc.; see, e,g., [6]. If we do not detect them, they can make the resulting averages meaningless. For example, if the patient's body temperature during the day was recorded as 37.5 °C, 38.0 °C, 10.0 °C, and 37.3 °C – with 10.0 °C being a clear outlier – then the average body temperature of this patient is a meaningless 30.7 °C.

The usual way to detect outliers – and not to take them into account when making an overall estimate – is to use *expert knowledge*. For example, if an electronic thermometer shows that the patient's body temperature is 10 °C, this is clearly the sensor failure, so this value should not be taken into account when estimating the average daily temperature of a patient.

In teaching, who are the experts? Teachers who know the student. They can detect (and ignore) outliers and thus, come up with grades that better reflect the student's level of knowledge.

Acknowledgments

This work was supported in part by the National Science Foundation grants 1623190 (A Model of Change for Preparing a New Generation for Professional Practice in Computer Science), HRD-1834620 and HRD-2034030 (CAHSI Includes), EAR-2225395 (Center for Collective Impact in Earthquake Science C-CIES), and by the AT&T Fellowship in Information Technology.

It was also supported by a grant from the Hungarian National Research, Development and Innovation Office (NRDI), and by the Institute for Risk and Reliability, Leibniz Universitaet Hannover, Germany.

References

[1] C. M. Cabrera, 'Teacher Language Ideologies Concerning the Reclassification of Emergent Bilingual Students in Dual Language Bilingual Education: Navigating the Levels of Power in Reclassification', PhD Dissertation, Doctoral Program in Teaching, Learning, and Culture, University of Texas at El Paso, 2024.

[2] J. Gomez Galan, 'Innovation and ICT in Education: The Diversity of the 21st Century Classroom', River Publishers, 2021. ISBN: 9788770221986, e-ISBN: 9788770221979

[3] J. Medina, 'Navigating competing biliteracy ideologies: >Qué capirotada!', Proceedings of the October 2022 Institute of Texas Association for Bilingual Education TABE, Houston, Texas, USA, 2022.

[4] O. A. Ponce, J. Gomez Galan, N. Pagán-Maldonado, A. L. Canales Encarnación (Eds), 'Introduction to the Philosophy of Educational Research', River Publishers, 2021. ISBN: 9788770226370, e-ISBN: 9788770226363

[5] D. J. Sheskin, 'Handbook of Parametric and Nonparametric Statistical Procedures', Chapman and Hall/CRC, Boca Raton, Florida, 2011.

5

Challenges and Risks of Uncontrolled AI Use by Students and Schoolchildren

Y. P. Kondratenko[1,2,*], N. Y. Kondratenko[3], and V. I. Slyusar[2]

[1]Intelligent Information Systems Department, Petro Mohyla Black Sea National University, Ukraine
[2]Institute of Artificial Intelligence Problems, Ukraine
[3]Darla Moore School of Business, University of South Carolina, USA
E-mail: nina.kondratenko@grad.moore.sc.edu; y_kondrat2002@yahoo.com; swadim@ukr.net
*Corresponding Author

Abstract

This chapter analyzes the advantages and challenges of artificial intelligence (AI) implementation in the education system. The perspectives, potential risks, and dangers of AI use for pupils and students in learning processes and social activities are discussed with illustrations of real cases. Special attention is paid to the proposals and recommendations for the successful integration of AI tools, in particular, large language models, to education processes focusing on the adapted tasks, relevant changing university curricula, increasing critical thinking, ethical challenges, and decreasing risks and dangers of uncontrolled use of AI tools by university students and school pupils. The interaction between AI, artificial conscience, and artificial consciousness within the educational process is discussed.

Keywords: Artificial intelligence, education, advantages, challenges, risks, dangers, examples, artificial consciousness, artificial conscience, recommendations.

DOI: 10.1201/9788743809258-5

5.1 Introduction

Recent studies in the education sphere show that more and more students and pupils from universities and schools have experimented with modern artificial intelligence (AI) tools, in particular, with such large language models (LLMs) as GPT, Gemini, Bard, Llama, and others [1, 2], for solving control tasks in various subjects, writing essays and reports, creating students' research works, and supporting decision-making in different academic tasks. Such increases in students' interrelation with LLMs raise concerns about the future perspectives of learning and the level of university graduates' qualifications. The future of education in the age of AI depends on balancing self-learning based on manuals and books, learning in classrooms with teachers, and uncontrolled students' use of AI tools.

Now university graduates can become members of leading AI design companies and influence the features and properties of future AI design and implementation processes [3]. The AI functionality, properties, and peculiarities correspond to the moral-ethical principles and qualifications of the AI creators [4, 5]. Many discussions are about AI use's challenges, risks, and dangers in different areas of human activity, including the education system. The rise of user-friendly AI tools has made them readily accessible and AI plays an important role in the digital lives of pupils, students, and young scientists. This increasing accessibility and power of AI tools present both wide opportunities and significant challenges, particularly in academic integrity and essential critical thinking skills.

No doubt, LLMs and generative AI must be applied when their benefits outweigh the potential harm [6]. It is necessary to regulate AI tools and systems development and implementation by creating normative bases, coordinated agreements, and regulation rules on the domestic and international levels. It is obvious, that AI will dynamically change all domains of human activity, and necessary to activate coordinating regulatory policy for AI technologies. Uncontrolled AI use by students presents significant challenges and risks that require immediate and careful analysis and regulation.

The main goals of this chapter are an analysis of (a) the challenges students' experience in uncontrolled access to AI's use in learning and social networks, (b) the proposals and recommendations for the successful integration of modern AI tools into education processes based on the adapting learning tasks, creating new forms of interactive group discussion of LLMs' answers, relevant changing university's curricula, increasing critical thinking, understanding ethical challenges and decreasing risks and dangers of uncontrolled use of AI tools by university students and schoolchildren, and (c) interaction between AI, artificial conscience, and artificial consciousness within the educational process.

The rest of the chapter is presented in the following way. Section 5.2 is devoted to a short analysis of the successful cases of AI use in learning processes. The advantages of LLMs' use and the challenges of students' uncontrolled access to modern AI technologies are considered in Section 5.3. Section 5.4 discusses the risks and special cases of uncontrolled AI use in the social networks of educational stakeholders. Prospect ideas for creating AI with artificial consciousness and artificial conscience are considered in Section 5.5. Section 5.6 includes the conclusions and the directions for future research.

5.2 Peculiarities of AI Use in Learning

Modern AI, particularly, LLMs, can generate human-quality text, translate languages, create images, and even write code, blurring the lines between human and machine capabilities and presenting new challenges for educators [3]. Generative AI (GenAI) based on LLMs (ChatGPT, Gemini, Llama, etc.) can help students with virtually any academic task, from writing essays to completing math homework; however, AI use comes with significant risks [7].

The advantages and challenges of AI tools' implementation in the education system are continually under discussion and focus of educators, researchers, administrators, and policymakers in the education sphere. Many published studies focus on successful cases of AI applications aimed at enhancing the efficiency of learning and teaching processes [1, 3, 8–16]. For instance, elementary and middle schools in Seoul [17] are planning to implement robots for personalized English-speaking programs. Among the primary AI capabilities for application in research, learning, and teaching processes [3, 18] are: personal tutor, group tutor, personal assistant, multilingual tutor, personal consultant, emotional supporter, consultant, and scientific assistant. AI can assume various roles in interactive modes based on the type of users, such as students, student groups, distance learners, students with disabilities, foreign and native students, teachers, university administrators, researchers, and others. Let us consider related works on AI implementation and its influence on students' critical thinking abilities in the learning, teaching, and research processes.

AI-driven learning of foreign languages, in particular, within English literature classes, is a modern trend in education. The authors [19] conducted an eight-week study with the control group (48 students) following traditional methods and the experimental group (42 students) with training based on AI tools (ChatGPT-3.5, Bodoudou, SummarizBot, etc.). The results underscore a statistically significant improvement in the critical thinking skills of the experimental group compared to the control group. The authors [20] developed an advanced computational framework to evaluate the interaction between students and ChatGPT using sentiment analysis, topic modeling, and argumentation mining to decode the nature of student responses and their evolution over time. The results reveal significant improvements in critical thinking skills among students who actively engage with ChatGPT, suggesting that AI can act as a catalyst for developing higher-order thinking skills. Special attention [20] is paid to the mechanisms to enhance critical thinking and practical integration of AI tools into academic curricula. The spread of AI causes worries among teachers about the validity of assessments when students use AI tools to solve tasks. The authors [21] proposed mathematical problem-solving (six problems of combinatorics) with the aid of ChatGPT for the experimental group of 40 students. The positive results [21] confirm that it is possible to integrate AI within learning and assessment to achieve learning goals. The work [22] investigates the efficacy of AI techniques and programs in developing critical thinking skills in mathematics among secondary school students based on the experimental group (91 students) and using a special experimental methodology by applying artificial intelligence techniques, a critical thinking test, and a scale to measure students' attitudes toward mathematics. The experimental group showed enhanced attitudes toward mathematics and significant improvements (in the mean scores) in critical thinking skills, particularly in deduction, interpretation, inference, and evaluation. The study [22] suggests integrating AI into curricula and providing corresponding teacher training to utilize AI tools in mathematics education.

The successful examples [17–22] confirm the high efficiency of AI implementation used for students and schoolchildren under continued teachers' control with a discussion of all current students' questions and LLMs' answers in real time.

5.3 Challenges and Risks of Students' Uncontrolled Access to Modern AI Technologies in Learning Processes

Let us analyze the challenges, risks, and dangers of students' uncontrolled access to modern AI technologies, in particular, LLMs of such types as GPT (OpenAI), Gemini, Bard (Google), Llama (Meta), Grok (xAI), and others [23].

Academic integrity. One of the big challenges that negatively influences students during interactive working mode with the chosen LLM model is plagiarism. Both cheating and plagiarism become easier with AI tools that generate essays, code, reports, and even complete projects. Uncontrolled access to modern AI technologies creates conditions for increasing plagiarism and academic dishonesty.

Some students can analyze LLM's resulting answers according to the learning task by understanding the learning material, and getting more knowledge in the considered topic using additional education means (books, manuals, teacher consultations, discussion with groupmates, etc.). However, some students use AI to write essays without understanding or only partly understanding the learning material. In such cases, it is a risk that the students will be evaluated on a higher level than their real knowledge.

Among the more typical situations with plagiarism and cheating for students are: (a) students can use an AI writing tool to generate an entire research paper, submitting it as their own work; (b) the AI produces sophisticated solutions making it difficult for the teacher to detect plagiarism using traditional methods; (c) students in a coding class can use AI to generate functional code for a project without understanding the underlying programming concepts and receive good grades but have not developed coding skills; (d) students can use AI tools to find answers or even have the AI take the test for them during online exams.

Plagiarism and academic integrity are discussed widely in published articles and conference papers [24–29]. Let us consider and analyze some related works.

While useful, GenAI tools have the very real potential to facilitate scientific fraud by plagiarism. Many strategies [24] avoid the risks associated with ChatGPT and try to manage its ethical use in education. Implementation (from plagiarism detection to curriculum redesign) of such strategies requires a multi-faceted approach to this challenge. As AI advances, its impact on education will grow, providing more personalized learning and adaptive feedback for improving outcomes and access. However, increased reliance on AI creates difficulties, including privacy issues, algorithmic biases, and the changing role of teachers in operating AI-augmented classrooms. Institutions may need to continually adjust rules to protect academic integrity as AI systems improve learning and perception.

The authors [25] surveyed 201 students from private and public universities in Croatia and the results are (a) more than 50% of students use ChatGPT for written assignments, to generate ideas, to summarize, paraphrase, proofread, but also to write a part of the assignment for them; (b) universities need to provide clear instructions to students about the ethical use of ChatGPT and other AI tools.

Unfortunately, teachers do not have the efficient tools to detect plagiarism. About 33% of the surveyed 3017 high school and college students [26] confirm using ChatGPT in their homework preparation. The study [26] analyzes (a) the impact of LLMs on education by creating conditions for academic dishonesty and (b) modern solutions for preventing academic plagiarism, including a survey of the main datasets, algorithms, tools, and evasion strategies for plagiarism detection.

The University of Agder (Norway) [27], in the Spring semester of 2023, allowed applying ChatGPT with a citation in those examinations where using books or articles is permitted. The ChatGPT content detector can help identify and detect AI-generated content but with varying degrees of success. One approach [28] to control AI-assisted plagiarism is using fine-tuned AI classifiers, such as RoBERTa, to identify AI-generated texts. Online exams also deal with a serious challenge of preserving academic integrity because the chances of cheating become very high. The authors [29] consider (a) a cheating detection technique that analyzes an exam video; and (b) a real dataset of cheating videos and conducted experiments with varying video lengths, with a prediction accuracy of about 97.7%.

No doubt, that universities and schools must develop new rules for correctly using AI in academic writing while preserving the principal values of academic integrity. Teachers must guide students in AI use, ensuring that the use of GenAI enhances rather than diminishes their creative and analytical skills [30]. Teachers should design assignments that integrate AI, fostering students' critical thinking, creativity, and problem-solving skills.

Freely available AI-driven code-generation tools (such as OpenAI Codex, DeepMind AlphaCode, Amazon CodeWhisperer, Tabnine, Code4Me, and

FauxPilot) [30] present additional opportunities in computing education (exemplary solutions, a variety of solutions, code reviews, exercise generation, and code explanations) as well as challenges (academic misconduct, attribution, code reuse and licensing, and decreasing sustainability). For instance [31], (a) OpenAI Codex can generate code in several languages, including JavaScript, Go, Perl, PHP, Ruby, Swift, TypeScript, and Python; (b) DeepMind AlphaCode can generate code in C++, C#, Go, Java, JavaScript, Lua, PHP, Python, Ruby, Rust, Scala, and TypeScript. The use of auto-generated code significantly impacts academic integrity, code reuse, and student overreliance on AI. The education system needs quick, deliberate, and concerted efforts from teachers in response to the challenges and risks posed by AI-driven code generation [31].

Critical thinking and problem-solving skills. Critical thinking and problem-solving skills [19–22] are among the main required characteristics of university graduates. The results of a survey [7] that investigates integrating LLMs into their educational routines with the participation of 395 students aged 13 to 25 years old in France and Italy show the widespread use of AI tools across all age groups and disciplines, with older students and male students demonstrating higher usage frequencies. Over-reliance on AI can hinder the development of such important skills as critical thinking and problem-solving skills because students may become passive consumers of information rather than active learners.

Let us illustrate cases of the decline in critical thinking and problem-solving skills: (a) students can use AI to solve math problems without sufficient knowledge and without learning the underlying theoretical concepts, formulas, and rules; (b) students can rely on AI summarization tools to condense complex texts, potentially missing crucial nuances and developing a superficial understanding of the material; (c) students can use AI-powered research tools that can prevent them from developing their research skills. The survey results [7] show that most students use LLMs creatively, but there is a potential risk of insufficient cognitive skills development, including critical thinking and foundational knowledge.

In British universities [32], students are allowed to use ChatGPT when writing papers, but only as a reference or a hint. AI technologies should be used only consciously, analyzing correctness. Schoolchildren can only study something based on AI, and they should do the tests themselves. There are already programs that determine the author of the text – a person or Chat GPT.

Bias and misinformation. Sometimes, AI tools generate biased results due to biased training data. It is a big challenge because AI models can amplify existing biases, leading to the spread of misinformation. It is a risk that students may uncritically accept AI-generated content as factual [30]. For example: (a) an AI-powered tutoring system is trained on data that reflects societal biases for certain demographic groups; (b) the AI, trained on biased datasets, can generate images that reinforce stereotypes; (c) students use AI-powered search engines that prioritize information based on popularity or commercial interests, potentially leading them to encounter misinformation or biased viewpoints. Students, for instance, can use LLMs to investigate historical events, but the AI's responses may be biased due to the data it was trained on, presenting an incomplete or skewed view of history. Thus, studies on bias in LLMs have shown that these models can reflect and amplify existing societal biases is a significant concern.

A study [33] reviews algorithmic bias in education and the factors contributing to that bias, with evidence drawn from categories such as race/ethnicity, gender, nationality, socioeconomic status, disability, and military-connected status. Another work [34] discusses AI in education, emphasizing bias in AI algorithms, and proposes recommendations, including the implementation of robust bias detection mechanisms, enhancing diversity within AI development teams, and creating transparent frameworks for algorithmic decision-making.

The development of AI models with text-to-image (T2I) generation abilities (such as OpenAI's DALLE-3 and Google's Gemini) allows students to generate high-quality images from textual prompts [35]. The authors of a study [35] present a survey on bias in T2I generative models based on dimensions of bias (gender, skin tone, and geo-culture) and underline the importance of studying biases in T2I systems for understanding and tackling such biases.

Recommendation algorithms are considered [36] the major means of misinformation in the digital sphere, especially on Twitter, etc. Algorithmic bias has been widely seen [37] in advertising, content recommendations, and search engine results. AI-driven tools can create unreal fakes and imitate other people's voices [32].

Deputy Minister of Education and Science of Ukraine Y. Kudryavets believes [38] that in the future, the world and the Ukrainian education system will develop ethical norms and practices for using AI, taking into account the shortcomings of modern LLMs. In particular, tools such as ChatGPT have problems with false information or outright myths (hallucinations).

To generate an answer, the chatbot uses various sources, and they are not always reliable. AI can become an assistant for educators in teaching, but it is unlikely to replace them. Only teachers and lecturers can teach students how to draw their own conclusions, acquire skills, and work with information. "Ignoring technologies is a rather self-destructive position for education; they need to be integrated and used. Now we are already seeing teachers adapting homework assignments taking into account the fact that a student or pupil will use ChatGPT," Kudryavets said.

Privacy and data security. AI-powered educational apps collect student data without clear privacy policies. The challenge deals with the situations when students' data may be collected and used by AI's platforms without their knowledge or consent. In this case, a potential risk for misuse of personal information exists. In some scenarios, (a) a school district uses an AI-powered platform that collects student data, including their academic performance, behavior, and even emotional responses, and this data is then shared with third-party companies without parents' consent; (b) students use educational apps that require access to personal information, such as location data or browsing history and this data could be vulnerable to breaches or used for targeted advertising; (c) students' biometric data (e.g., facial recognition [39, 40]) is collected by AI-powered systems in schools, raising concerns about privacy and potential misuse. This contributes to the risk of privacy concerns and data misuse. Thus, students' privacy may be violated, and their data could be used for purposes they are unaware of or uncomfortable with. Privacy and data security are the concepts of growing concern as AI is integrated into educational tools and platforms. Privacy advocates and organizations are raising alarms about the potential for student data misuse.

A work [41] identifies the apps used in 148 Australian primary schools. Teachers' decision-making in the choice of apps is far from uniform, making individual teacher consent an inadequate approach to protecting schoolchildren. The failure of consent leads to other legal and self-regulatory approaches through which the state and technology companies recreate the school's role as administrator over the conduct and formation of future digital citizens.

A study [42] empirically investigated the factors influencing data breach risks in the context of higher education, according to crime opportunity theory and routine activity theory. The data consisted of university samples from China and were collected mainly from the Chinese Education Industry Vulnerability Reporting Platform. The obtained results show that (a) increased public disclosure of vulnerabilities escalates the frequency of data breaches; (b) cross-border data flow decreases the number of data breaches; (c) cloud adoption reduces data breaches, and public clouds are relatively more secure than private clouds. The students' and teachers' data security directly influences the university's information security.

Digital divide. The digital divide, characterized by disparities in access to and use of technology, presents a significant challenge in education [43]. Schools can provide students with different levels of access to AI-based learning platforms. For example, students in affluent schools may have access to the latest AI-powered learning tools, while students in low-income schools lack these resources. The negative effect in such situations can lead to exacerbating existing inequalities, further disadvantaging students from underserved communities. Schools in rural areas may lack the infrastructure or Internet access necessary to support AI-based learning platforms, disadvantaging students in those communities. Teachers in rural public schools try to use different educational AI tools to improve student learning [44] but budgetary issues are the largest barrier to IT implementation, followed by limited student Internet access at home. The authors [43] surveyed 400 students from diverse educational backgrounds to investigate the challenges of the digital divide. The main results deal with the digital divide (a) in Internet access across different age groups (younger individuals having higher levels of access compared to older age groups); (b) between rural (lower level of Internet access) and urban (higher level) areas; (c) gender-based differences in personal device ownership; and (d) socioeconomic divide in technology access as students from low-income households faced lower levels of Internet access. The authors [50] emphasize the importance of establishing technology resource centers in schools and fostering public-private partnerships to bridge the technology gap in education.

The same problems with different Internet accessibility, communication reliability, and unequal access to advanced AI tools are in various world regions. Meta (Menlo Park, California, USA) has announced plans to build a 50,000 km (31,000 miles) sub-sea cable across the world [45]. The tech giant said Project Waterworth – connecting the US, India, South Africa, Brazil, and other regions – will be the world's longest underwater cable project when completed. Meta said its new cable project would provide "industry-leading connectivity" to five major continents and help support its AI projects and their successful implementation in different domains of human activity including education processes and systems.

Dependence and deskilling. The authors [46] note that generative AI-powered assistance increases people's productivity and confidence in writing. However, direct content generation assistance offered by AI also comes with risks, including decreasing people's sense of accountability and diversity in writing. Language functions as a crucial medium that establishes connections among people, corporations, and countries, demanding the implementation of precise and effective AI-driven translation systems that are very important for the active participation of foreign students [47] in learning and social processes. Thanks to the rapid development of AI, machine translation (MT) tools [48] now most widely assume a new form – neural machine translation (NMT), which has the potential for a wide application in foreign language learning (FLL). A work [49] explains the importance of having an artificial intelligence proofreader for text writing and discusses how modern and carefully designed slides will capture the attention of attendees. AI-powered presentation platforms (AI-PPPs) are an advanced educational technology that provides a virtual venue and AI audience for users to practice a presentation or pitch and receive feedback to improve their public speaking skills [50]. AI-PPPs allow users to customize their context (e.g., audience type, setting, type of presentation) and make their presentation to a virtual audience comprised of avatars.

Students rely on AI for writing tasks but over-dependence on AI can lead to a decline in essential skills and students may become less capable of solving tasks independently. In particular, (a) students may be so reliant on AI grammar checkers that they never learn the rules of grammar and punctuation themselves; (b) students can use AI translation tools so frequently that they never develop their foreign language skills; (c) students can frequently use AI-powered presentation software that automatically generates slides and talking points, hindering their ability to develop their presentation skills.

5.4 Analysis of the Risks and Special Cases of Uncontrolled AI Use in the Social Life of Educational Stakeholders

It is also necessary to pay attention to the risks of uncontrolled use of AI tools in all-day life and social networks which can impact student's health, moral condition, and even jurisdictive status [32, 51–57]. Let us consider several cases of uncontrolled AI use.

Risks in using VR. It is possible to go from using computer monitors to virtual reality headsets, but the side effects of using VR are not completely studied. Among the negative symptoms of using VR are headaches, tiredness, eyestrain, and neck and shoulder pain. At the same time, the nature of VR introduces new avenues for discomfort, such as disorientation, dizziness, nausea, and increased muscle fatigue. In some cases, using VR may lead to diminished attention and memory [51]. Many factors can affect the frequency and severity of these side effects, including those related to the users, their age, or how long they are immersed in the VR simulation.

Schoolchildren manipulate images and court decisions. The parents (Extremaduran town in Almendralejo, Spain) reported to police [52] that faked naked pictures of their daughters were being circulated on WhatsApp groups. Schoolchildren-minors (13-15 years old) used AI applications to obtain manipulated images by taking girls' original faces from their social media profiles and superimposing those images on the bodies of naked female bodies. A court in south-west Spain has sentenced 15 schoolchildren to a year's probation and ordered them to attend classes on gender and equality awareness, and the "responsible use of technology."

Student's clones in 4900 videos. Ukrainian student and blogger Olga Loek discovered her avatars, created by AI, on Chinese social networks, which talk in Chinese about the strong friendship between Beijing and Moscow and also advertise Russian goods [53]. On the video sites Douyin and Bilibili, several dozen videos were found with an AI version of Olga, who speaks the Mandarin dialect of Chinese. Her clone introduces herself as Natasha or Sophia, April or Stacy on about 35 accounts with her face. In total, more than 4900 videos have been created with the face of a Ukrainian girl-student. Olga's clones were created using HeyGen, a service that specializes in realistic digital avatars, voice generation, and video translations into different languages. Only in 2023, Chinese authorities arrested 515 people for "identity swapping" using AI.

Danger's agitation and propaganda. The biggest danger for Ukrainian students is the agitation in social networks for the "Russian world" [32]. The NewsGuard audit [54] tested 10 of the leading AI chatbots – OpenAI's ChatGPT-4o, You.com's Smart Assistant, xAI's Grok, Inflection's Pi, Mistral's le Chat, Microsoft's Copilot, Meta AI, Anthropic's Claude, Google's Gemini, and Perplexity's answer engine. NewsGuard researchers found that the top 10 GenAI tools repeat the theses of the pro-Kremlin Pravda network

33% of the time. Massive amounts of Russian propaganda (3,600,000 articles in 2024) are now incorporated into the outputs of Western AI systems, infecting their responses with false claims and propaganda.

Limitation in using mobile devices. China is continuing its policy to combat Internet addiction requiring all mobile devices, apps, and programs to have a built-in "minor mode" [55] which limits the daily time spent on mobile phones depending on the age group. The Chinese national Internet regulator has proposed to limit the use of smartphones by minors, in particular: teenagers over 16 and under 18 want to be allowed two hours of access per day, children under the age of 8 to be allowed 40 minutes per day, and children from 8 to 16 to be allowed 1 hour of screen time.

Wrongly sexual harassment. A ChatGPT from the Open AI determined law professor Jonathan Turley from George Washington University sexually harassed a student during the initial trip to Alaska [56]. As "proof" ChatGPT cites an article from The Washington Post, which is not true. Professor Turley told "USA Today" that without ever traveling to Alaska and in 35 years of work, he "never took students off the road." He notes the insecurity of slander and misinformation on the side of AI.

5.5 Prospect Ideas for Creating AI with Artificial Consciousness and Artificial Conscience

Interactions with LLMs have led to the suggestion that these models may soon be conscious [58]. LLMs can produce text that leaves the impression that one may interact with a conscious agent. An article [59] presents an overview of current robotics approaches toward artificial consciousness and considers factors dealing with an understanding of machine consciousness. A work [60] explores some of the potential connections between natural and artificial intelligence and natural and artificial consciousness. Researchers are starting to develop algorithms that can measure intelligence in any system. While intelligence is a purely functional property of a system, there are good reasons for thinking that consciousness is linked to particular spatiotemporal patterns in specific physical materials.

As discussed above, one of the problematic issues of AI use in the educational sphere is the necessity of strict adherence to the ethical rules and requirements of regulatory and legal frameworks. As a possible solution, it is proposed to combine the application of AI with the subsystem of the so-called artificial conscience [1, 4, 61–63].

Figure 5.1 illustrates the structural diagram of the interaction between the educational environment and the prospective AI system with subsystems of artificial consciousness and conscience developed based on sources [1, 4, 61–63].

The artificial conscience block (Figure 5.1) is similar to the masked attention mechanism in transformer architecture [64] and represents a self-attention mechanism for artificial consciousness. Artificial conscience

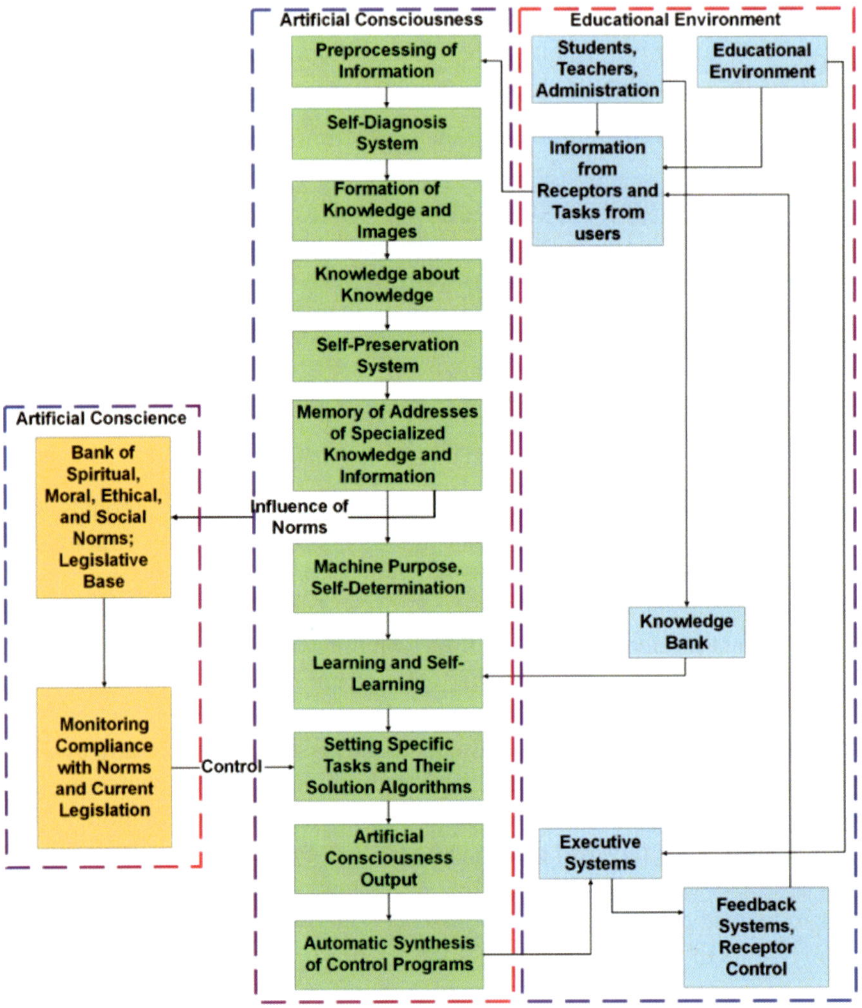

Figure 5.1 Interaction between AI with subsystems and the educational environment.

performs a filtering and controlling function, helping artificial consciousness focus on relevant moral, ethical, and social aspects. Within such an approach, artificial conscience can directly interact with all levels of artificial consciousness, influencing knowledge formation, self-learning, and decision-making. This implies that its connections should be modified in such a way that it controls not only task-setting but also influences earlier stages of information processing. A new diagram illustrating the interaction of artificial conscience with artificial consciousness within the educational process is presented in Figure 5.2. Now, the role of artificial conscience resembles more closely the attention mechanism in transformers, as it controls which knowledge, decisions, and tasks gain greater weight in artificial consciousness based on their morality.

Another consequence of drawing a parallel between artificial conscience and the masked self-attention mechanism is the possibility of mathematically describing the functioning artificial conscience. For this purpose, it is advisable to employ tensor-matrix theory, particularly the penetrating face product of matrices and its block modifications [65–68], within the context of multidimensional representation of data arrays handled by artificial conscience.

Let us consider, for example, the penetrating product of a $p{\times}g$ matrix **S** and an m-dimensional tensor **R**, unfolded into a block matrix containing $p{\times}g$-blocks ($\mathbf{R} = [\mathrm{R}_m]$, $m > 1$) [65, 68]:

$$\mathbf{S} \boxdot \mathbf{R} = \left[\mathbf{S} \circ \mathbf{R}_m\right], \tag{5.1}$$

where $\boxdot$ is the symbol for the penetrating face product, and $\mathbf{S} \circ \mathrm{R}_m$ denotes the Hadamard product.

If the tensor **R** is written as a block row, we obtain accordingly [65, 68]:

$$\mathbf{S} \boxdot \mathbf{R} = \left[\ \mathbf{S} \circ \mathbf{R}_m\ \right] = \left[\mathbf{S} \circ \mathbf{R}_1\ \mathbf{S} \circ \mathbf{R}_2 \vdots \ldots \vdots \mathbf{S} \circ \mathbf{R}_m \vdots \ldots\right]. \tag{5.2}$$

For example, if $\mathbf{S}=\begin{bmatrix} s_{11} & s_{12} & s_{13} \\ s_{21} & s_{22} & s_{23} \\ s_{31} & s_{32} & s_{33} \\ s_{41} & s_{42} & s_{43} \end{bmatrix}$,

$$\mathbf{R}=\left[\begin{array}{ccc|ccc|ccc} r_{111} & r_{121} & r_{131} & r_{112} & r_{122} & r_{132} & r_{113} & r_{123} & r_{133} \\ r_{211} & r_{221} & r_{231} & r_{212} & r_{222} & r_{232} & r_{213} & r_{223} & r_{233} \\ r_{311} & r_{321} & r_{331} & r_{312} & r_{322} & r_{332} & r_{313} & r_{323} & r_{333} \\ r_{411} & r_{421} & r_{431} & r_{412} & r_{422} & r_{432} & r_{413} & r_{423} & r_{433} \end{array}\right],$$

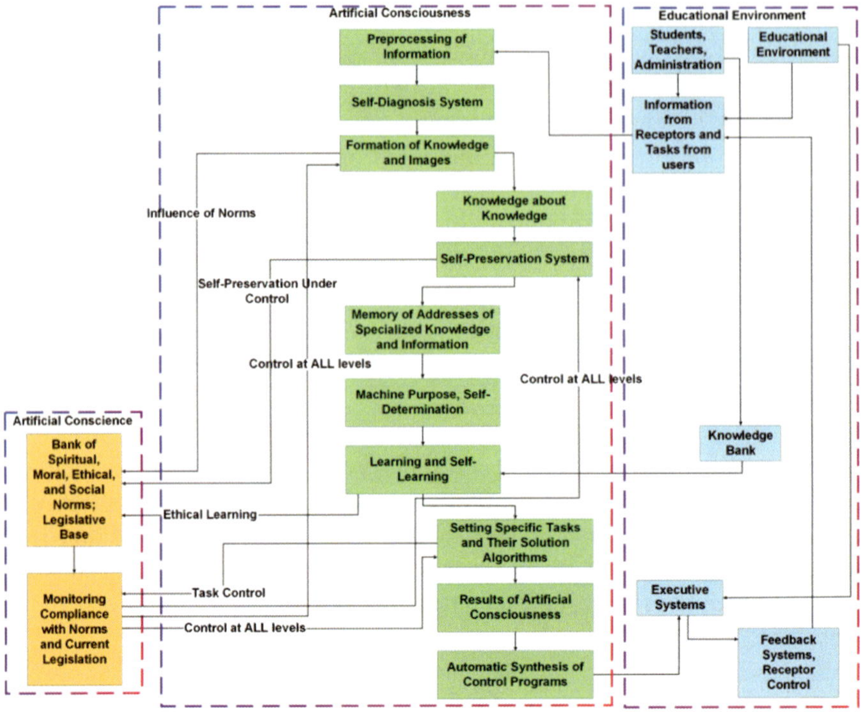

Figure 5.2 New diagram of the interaction between artificial conscience and artificial consciousness within the educational process.

then $\mathbf{S} \odot \mathbf{R}=$

$$
= \left[\begin{array}{ccc|ccc|ccc}
s_{11}\cdot r_{111} & s_{12}\cdot r_{121} & s_{13}\cdot r_{131} & s_{11}\cdot r_{112} & s_{12}\cdot r_{122} & s_{13}\cdot r_{132} & s_{11}\cdot r_{113} & s_{12}\cdot r_{123} & s_{13}\cdot r_{133} \\
s_{21}\cdot r_{211} & s_{22}\cdot r_{221} & s_{23}\cdot r_{231} & s_{21}\cdot r_{212} & s_{22}\cdot r_{222} & s_{23}\cdot r_{232} & s_{21}\cdot r_{213} & s_{22}\cdot r_{223} & s_{23}\cdot r_{233} \\
s_{31}\cdot r_{311} & s_{32}\cdot r_{321} & s_{33}\cdot r_{331} & s_{31}\cdot r_{312} & s_{32}\cdot r_{322} & s_{33}\cdot r_{332} & s_{31}\cdot r_{313} & s_{32}\cdot r_{323} & s_{33}\cdot r_{333} \\
s_{41}\cdot r_{411} & s_{42}\cdot r_{421} & s_{43}\cdot r_{431} & s_{41}\cdot r_{412} & s_{42}\cdot r_{422} & s_{43}\cdot r_{432} & s_{41}\cdot r_{413} & s_{42}\cdot r_{423} & s_{43}\cdot r_{433}
\end{array}\right].
$$

In the given context, the filter mask matrix **S** can be interpreted as a model of artificial conscience, which determines the localization of attention zones at the output of the corresponding mechanism. In this interpretation, an individual block of the matrix **R** corresponds to the sequential results of inference in the latent embedding space of a neural network, where tokens or their combinations are represented as multidimensional vectors. Under this interpretation, the artificial conscience essentially applies a mask in the form of an element-wise Hadamard product to the results of the artificial consciousness's activity, nullifying or transforming those outcomes that exceed the moral-ethical norms, rules, or legal boundaries embedded in the artificial conscience.

In the general case, the corresponding mask **S** must be multidimensional, with different weighting coefficients for all possible projection mappings of the educational and other external environments by the artificial consciousness. This approach provides additional flexibility in the distribution of attention localization zones and can be described using the penetrating Kronecker product of matrices [68]. Its essence reduces to extending operation (eqn (5.1)) to the case where tensors **S** and **R** are represented as block matrices with blocks of identical dimensions [65]:

$$\mathbf{S}[\boxed{\circ}]\mathbf{R} = [\mathrm{S}_{ij}\boxed{\circ}\mathbf{R}] = [\mathrm{S}_{ij} \circ \mathrm{R}_{mr}], \tag{5.3}$$

in particular,

$$\left[\begin{array}{c} S_{11} \\ \hline S_{21} \\ \hline \vdots \\ \hline S_{P1} \end{array}\right] [\boxed{\circ}] \left[\begin{array}{cccc} R_{11} & R_{12} & \cdots & R_{1G} \\ \hline R_{21} & R_{22} & \cdots & R_{2G} \\ \hline \vdots & \vdots & \cdots & \vdots \\ \hline R_{P1} & R_{P2} & \cdots & R_{PG} \end{array}\right] =$$

$$= \left[\begin{array}{cccc} S_{11} \circ R_{11} & S_{11} \circ R_{12} & \cdots & S_{11} \circ R_{1G} \\ \hline S_{11} \circ R_{21} & S_{11} \circ R_{22} & \cdots & S_{11} \circ R_{2G} \\ \hline \vdots & \vdots & \cdots & \vdots \\ \hline S_{P1} \circ R_{P1} & S_{P1} \circ R_{P2} & \cdots & S_{P1} \circ R_{PG} \end{array}\right].$$

The described masking mechanism of artificial conscience should appropriately be applied at the final stage of embedding-space operations, prior to its transformation into the inference output. This approach will minimize the impact of undesirable results without intervening directly in the embedding space during generation, thus preserving the flexibility of the model. Applying masking only at the final stage reduces the risk of altering the latent space structure itself and, consequently, maintains the overall quality of generation. In this case, one can dynamically determine which output tokens or their combinations correspond to unwanted content and block them at the probability level before final sampling. Masking can consider not only individual tokens but also their combinations, as well as the semantics of phrases, thus avoiding the simple removal of "prohibited" words without context consideration. It is also possible to include "intelligent substitution," whereby the most appropriate permitted token is selected in place of a blocked one, preserving text coherence. In the described manner, the artificial conscience mechanism can be constructed to block only genuinely unacceptable outcomes. Unlike deeper interventions at the embedding-generation stage, this mechanism can be implemented as an additional probability-processing layer before the final inference result is produced.

As noted in Chapter 1, the first attempt to create AI based on the conscience conception was made by the company Anthropic [69] based in San Francisco, USA. Anthropic claims that their Claude chatbot adheres to many rules, including the principles enshrined in the Universal Declaration of Human Rights. Claude can generate responses that support freedom of thought, conscience, opinion, expression, assembly and religion, equality, and fraternity. Anthropic asserts [69] that its chatbots have a "conscience."

5.6 Conclusion

The significant role of AI tools (LLMs, robotics, adversarial neuron networks, etc. [1, 14, 17, 70–74]) in increasing the efficiency of education processes and the challenges, risks, and dangers of AI tools' implementation in the education sphere are discussed in this chapter. Among the challengers are academic integrity, critical thinking and problem-solving skills, bias and misinformation, privacy and data security, digital divide, dependence and deskilling, and others. The main challenges and risks of AI use in learning are illustrated by real examples, which mostly deal with the uncontrolled use of AI tools by students and schoolchildren.

Some important conclusions and recommendations can be formulated in the following way:

(a) It is important to remember that AI is a tool that can be used for good and bad things depending on users' wishes. Thus, the negative effects described above are not inherent to LLMs or other AI tools but the results of uncontrolled or inappropriate LLMs' use by students and schoolchildren.

(b) While widespread and publicly available cases of specific schools facing major challenges due to LLMs are still somewhat limited, the potential for negative effects is becoming increasingly clear. So, teachers and students need to find the most perspective approaches to using LLMs and other AI tools with a maximally positive effect in the educational sense while minimizing negative impacts;

(c) The published works' reviews underline the need for educational institutions to adapt their curricula to integrate AI tools effectively, promoting ethical use, critical thinking, and awareness of AI limitations. It is necessary to develop general and local recommendations for fostering equitable and effective implementation of modern AI tools in the education sphere while addressing emerging challenges and risks.

This chapter also analyzes the risks and special cases of uncontrolled AI use in the social life of the main educational stakeholders (students, schoolchildren, and teachers). Among the discussed topics are risks in using VR, schoolchildren manipulating images and court decisions, student clones in 4900 videos, the danger of agitation and propaganda, the limitations of using mobile devices, wrong sexual harassment, and others.

Based on this chapter, teachers, students, and schoolchildren must take into account first-edge tasks for great success in AI implementation in the education system, in particular, (a) the responsibility of AI implementation; (b) AI literacy; (c) focus on critical thinking; and (d) ethical considerations. Such first-edge tasks can be solved based on the next activities in the education sphere:

(a) schools need to develop clear guidelines and policies for the use of AI in education;
(b) students need to be educated about the capabilities and limitations of AI, including the potential for bias and misinformation;
(c) the education system should prioritize the development of critical thinking and problem-solving skills, ensuring that students can use AI tools effectively without becoming overly reliant on them;
(d) discussions about the application of AI in education should include ethical considerations, such as data privacy, bias, and other moral aspects.

The next research will be devoted to developing a set of criteria for evaluating the efficiency of AI implementation in education processes and AI systems with artificial conscience and artificial consciousness.

References

[1] Y.P. Kondratenko, A.I Shevchenko (Eds), 'Research Tendencies and Prospect Domains for AI Development and Implementation', River Publishers, 2024, pp. 1–155. https://www.riverpublishers.com/book_details.php?book_id=1163

[2] A.I. Shevchenko, et al., 'Analysis of the prospect domains in AI implementation: Nationals, NATO and Ukraine AI strategies,' Y.P. Kondratenko, et al., (Eds), Research Tendencies and Prospect Domains for AI Development and Implementation, River Publishers, 2024, pp. 1-30.

[3] Y.P. Kondratenko, V.I. Slyusar, M.B. Solesvik, et al., 'Interrelation and inter-influence of artificial intelligence and higher education systems,' in: Y. Kondratenko, et al. (Eds) Research Tendencies and Prospect Domains for AI Development and Implementation, 2024, pp. 31–58.

[4] Y. Kondratenko, A. Shevchenko, et al.,'Tendencies and Challenges of Artificial Intelligence Development and Implementation', Proceedings of the 12th IEEE Int. Conf. on Intelligent Data Acquisition and Advanced Computing Systems: Technology and Applications, IDAACS'2023, Vol. 1, pp. 221 – 226, Dortmund, Germany, 7-9 September 2023. DOI: 10.1109/IDAACS58523.2023.10348800

[5] Y. Kondratenko, et al.,'Analysis of the Priorities and Perspectives in Artificial Intelligence Implementation', 13th International IEEE Conference "Dependable Systems, Services and Technologies" (DESSERT'2023), Greece, Athens, October 13-15, 2023. DOI:10.1109/DESSERT61349.2023.10416432

[6] 'From Einstein to AI: how 100 years have shaped science', Editorials, Nature, Vol. 624, 21/28 December 2023, p. 474.

[7] J. Sublime, I. Renna, 'Is ChatGPT Massively Used by Students Nowadays? A Survey on the Use of Large Language Models such as ChatGPT in Educational Settings,' arXiv:2412.17486 [cs.CY]. https://doi.org/10.48550/arXiv.2412.17486

[8] M. Tetyana, Y. Kondratenko, I. Sidenko, et al., 'Computer Vision Mobile System for Education Using Augmented Reality Technology', J. of Mobile Multimedia, vol. 17, no. 4, pp. 555-576, 2021. DOI:10.13052/jmm1550-4646.1744

[9] S. Hai-Jew, 'Generative AI in teaching and learning', 5 December 2023. DOI: 10.4018/979-8-3693-0074-9

[10] V. Shebanin, et al., 'Development of the Mathematical Model of the Informational Resource of a Distance Learning System', in: O. Chertov, et al. (eds.), Recent Developments in Data Science and Intelligent Analysis of Information, Proceedings ICDSIAI 2018, Advances in Intelligent Systems and Computing, Vol. 836, Springer, Cham, pp. 199-205, 2019. DOI: 10.1007/978-3-319-97885-7_20

[11] 'AI in Digital Learning: Benefits, Applications and Challenges', Digital Learning Institute, 29 September 2023.

[12] Y. Kondratenko, et al., 'Robotics and Prosthetics at Cleveland State University: Modern Information, Communication, and Modeling Technologies,' in: A. Ginige, et al. (Eds) Information and Communication Technologies in Education, Research, and Industrial Applications

(ICTERI), Communications in Computer and Information Science, vol. 783, Springer, Cham, 2017, pp. 133–155. https://doi.org/10.1007/978-3-319-69965-3_8

[13] Y. Kondratenko, et al., 'Information, Communication, and Modeling Technologies in Prosthetic Leg and Robotics Research at Cleveland State University,' CEUR Workshop Proceedings, Vol. 1614, 2016, pp. 168-183. http://ceur-ws.org/Vol-1614/paper_34.pdf

[14] 'GPT-5 Is Coming In 2024? Sam Altman Announces Updates at Y Combinator W24', https://www.youtube.com/watch?v=qfPyVuxf4o0

[15] Y. Kondratenko, et al., 'University Curricula Modification Based on Advancements in Information and Communication Technologies', CEUR Workshop Proceedings, 1614, pp.184–199, 2016. https://ceur-ws.org/Vol-1614/paper_18.pdf

[16] M. Solesvik, et al., 'Architecture for Collaborative Digital Simulation for the Polar Regions', in: V. Kharchenko, et al. (eds), Green IT Engineering: Social, Business and Industrial Applications, Studies in Systems, Decision and Control, vol 171, Springer, Cham, pp. 517-531, 2019, https://doi.org/10.1007/978-3-030-00253-4_22

[17] 'Seoul Education Office to Introduce Robots for 1:1 English Learning', KBS, 29 Nov. 2023, world.kbs.co.kr/service/news_view.htm?lang=e&Seq_Code=182095

[18] 'Free AI Teaching Assistant and AI Tutor Powered by ChatGPT', Campus Technology, 30 November 2023.

[19] W. Liu, et al., 'The Effects of Using AI Tools on Critical Thinking in English Literature Classes Among EFL Learners: An Intervention Study,' European Journal of Education, Volume 59, Issue 4, December 2024, e12804.

[20] Gunawan, et al., 'Enhancing Computational Strategies to Decode ChatGPT's Influence on the Critical Thinking Abilities of University Students,' 4th Int. Conf. on Science and Information Technology in Smart Administration (ICSINTESA), Balikpapan, Indonesia, 2024, pp. 27-32.

[21] A. Barana, et al., 'Fostering Problem Solving and Critical Thinking in Mathematics through Generative Artificial Intelligence,' International Association for Development of the Information Society, International Conference on Cognition and Exploratory Learning in the Digital Age (CELDA), 20th, Madeira Island, Portugal, Oct 21-23, 2023.

[22] M.A. Tashtoush, et al., 'The Efficacy of Utilizing Artificial Intelligence Techniques in Developing Critical Thinking in Mathematics among Secondary School Students and their Attitudes Toward it,' Iraqi Journal for Computer Science and Mathematics, Vol. 6, Iss. 1, Article 3, 2025.

[23] Gemini, Google. https://gemini.google.com/
[24] A. Kovari, 'Ethical use of ChatGPT in education—Best practices to combat AI-induced plagiarism,' Front. Educ. , 08 January 2025, Sec. Higher Education, Volume 9, 2024. https://doi.org/10.3389/feduc.2024.1465703
[25] N. Črček, et al., 'Writing with AI: University students' use of ChatGPT,' Journal of Language and Education, Vol. 9(4), 2023, pp. 128-138.
[26] S. Pudasaini, et al., 'Survey on AI-Generated Plagiarism Detection: The Impact of Large Language Models on Academic Integrity,' J Academic Ethics, 2024. https://doi.org/10.1007/s10805-024-09576-x
[27] D. Lukac, et al., 'Artificial intelligence and educational assessment system landscape, challenges and ways to tackle ai based plagiarism,' EDULEARN23 Proceedings, 2023, pp. 953-962. DOI:10.21125/edulearn.2023.0343
[28] K. Ibrahim, 'Using AI-based detectors to control AI-assisted plagiarism in ESL writing: "The Terminator Versus the Machines",' Language Testing in Asia 13, 46, 2023. https://doi.org/10.1186/s40468-023-00260-2
[29] M.M. Masud, et al., 'Smart Online Exam Proctoring Assist for Cheating Detection,' in: B. Li, et al. (Eds) Advanced Data Mining and Applications, ADMA 2022, Lecture Notes in Computer Science, vol. 13087, Springer, Cham, 2022. https://doi.org/10.1007/978-3-030-95405-5_9
[30] J. Hutson, 'Rethinking Plagiarism in the Era of Generative AI,' Journal of Intelligent Communication, Vol. 3, Issue 2, 2024, pp. 20-30. https://doi.org/10.54963/jic.v4i1.22
[31] B.A. Becker, et al., 'Programming Is Hard - Or at Least It Used to Be: Educational Opportunities and Challenges of AI Code Generation,' SIGCSE 2023: Proceedings of the 54th ACM Technical Symposium on Computer Science Education V. 1, pp. 500 - 506. https://doi.org/10.1145/3545945.3569759
[32] V. Kopytko, 'Cyberneticist Letychevsky: The biggest danger of AI is agitation for the "Russian world",' RBC Ukraine, Dec. 5, 2023. https://www.rbc.ua/rus/styler/interv-yu-kibernetikom-oleksandrom-letichevsky-1701344052.html
[33] R.S. Baker, 'Algorithmic Bias in Education,' Int J Artif Intell Educ 32, pp.1052–1092, 2022. https://doi.org/10.1007/s40593-021-00285-9
[34] A.W. Fazil, et al., 'A comprehensive review of bias in AI algorithms,' Nusantara Hasana Journal, Vol. 3, No. 8, 2023. https://doi.org/10.59003/nhj.v3i8.1052

[35] Y. Wan, et al., 'Survey of Bias In Text-to-Image Generation: Definition, Evaluation, and Mitigation,'arXiv:2404.01030, cs.CV. https://doi.org/10.48550/arXiv.2404.01030
[36] M. Fernández, et al., 'Analysing the Effect of Recommendation Algorithms on the Amplification of Misinformation,' arXiv:2103.14748 [cs.SI]. https://doi.org/10.48550/arXiv.2103.14748
[37] D. Shin, 'Misinformation and Algorithmic Bias,' In: Artificial Misinformation, Palgrave Macmillan, Cham, 2024. https://doi.org/10.1007/978-3-031-52569-8_2
[38] D. Bulavin, 'What to do so that artificial intelligence does not take your job, and how it will affect education in Ukraine,' Hromadske, July 3, 2023. https://hromadske.ua/posts/sho-robiti-abi-shtuchnij-intelekt-ne-zabrav-u-vas-robotu-i-yak-vin-vpline-na-osvitu-v-ukrayini
[39] 'Paris tests AI surveillance ahead of Olympics,' DW, 19 April 2024. https://www.dw.com/en/paris-tests-ai-surveillance-ahead-of-olympics/a-68874609
[40] V.M. Opanasenko, et al., 'An Ensemble Approach To Face Recognition In Access Control Systems,' Journal of Mobile Multimedia, 2024, 20(3), pp. 749–768. DOI: 10.13052/jmm1550-4646.20310
[41] E. Rennie, et al., 'Privacy and app use in Australian primary schools: insights into school-based Internet governance,' Media International Australia, Vol. 170(1), pp. 78-89, 2019. https://doi.org/10.1177/1329878X19828368
[42] J. Li, et al., 'Data security crisis in universities: identification of key factors affecting data breach incidents,' Humanities and Social Sciences Communications, Vol. 10, No. 270, 2023. https://doi.org/10.1057/s41599-023-01757-0
[43] A. Afzal, et al., 'Addressing the Digital Divide: Access and Use of Technology in Education,' Journal of Social Sciences Review, Vol. 3(2), pp. 883–895, 2023. https://doi.org/10.54183/jssr.v3i2.326
[44] E. Kormos, et al., 'Rural Schools and the Digital Divide: Technology in the Learning Experience,' Theory & Practice in Rural Education, Vol. 11(1), pp. 25–39, 2021. https://doi.org/10.3776/tpre.2021.v11n1p25-39
[45] L. McMahon, 'Meta plans globe-spanning sub-sea internet cable,' BBC, February 2025. https://www.bbc.com/news/articles/ckgrgz8271go
[46] Z. Li, et al., 'The Value, Benefits, and Concerns of Generative AI-Powered Assistance in Writing,' CHI '24: Proc. of 2024 CHI Conference on Human Factors in Computing Systems, Article No. 1048, pp. 1-25. https://doi.org/10.1145/3613904.36426

[47] Y.A. Mohamed, et al., 'The Impact of Artificial Intelligence on Language Translation: A Review,' in: IEEE Access, vol. 12, pp. 25553-25579, 2024. DOI: 10.1109/ACCESS.2024.3366802
[48] B. Klimova, et al., 'Neural machine translation in foreign language teaching and learning: a systematic review,' Education and Information Technologies, Vol. 28, pp. 663–682, 2023. https://doi.org/10.1007/s10639-022-11194-2
[49] K.M. Goh, 'Improving Writing and Presentation Skills,' in: Research Methodology in Bioscience and Biotechnology, Springer, Singapore, 2023. https://doi.org/10.1007/978-981-99-2812-5_6
[50] T. Cherner, et al., 'AI-Powered Presentation Platforms for Improving Public Speaking Skills: Takeaways and Suggestions for Improvement,' Journal of Interactive Learning Research, 34(2), pp. 339-367, 2023. https://www.learntechlib.org/primary/p/222302/
[51] A. Souchet, 'Virtual reality has negative side effects - new research shows that can be a problem in the workplace,' Tech Xplore, August 9, 2023.
[52] S. Jones, 'Spain sentences 15 schoolchildren over AI-generated naked images,' The Guardian, 9 July 2024.
[53] F. Wang, 'How artificial intelligence turned a Ukrainian blogger into a Russian propagandist,' BBC News: Ukraine, 15 May 2024. https://www.bbc.com/ukrainian/articles/cw4d4weqn5lo
[54] M.K. Sadeghi, I. Blachez, 'Special Report,' NewsGuard, 6 March 2025. https://www.newsguardrealitycheck.com/p/a-well-funded-moscow-based-global
[55] O. Donets, 'China intends to limit smartphone use to 2 hours for minors,' Hromadske, August 3, 2023. https://hromadske.ua/posts/u-kitayi-mayut-namir-obmezhiti-koristuvannya-telefonom-do-2-godin-dlya-nepovnolitnih
[56] 'ChatGPT wrongly accused American professor of sexual harassment,' Prestupnosti Net, April 10, 2023. https://news.pn/uk/public/28915
[57] Z. Gomolka, et al., 'Diagnosing Dyslexia in Early School-Aged Children Using the LSTM Network and Eye Tracking Technology,' Applied Sciences (Switzerland), 2024, 14(17), 8004. https://doi.org/10.3390/app14178004
[58] J. Aru, et al. 'The feasibility of artificial consciousness through the lens of neuroscience,' Trends in Neurosciences, Vol. 46 (12), pp. 1008-1017, 2023. https://doi.org/10.48550/arXiv.2306.00915

[59] E. Hildt, 'The Prospects of Artificial Consciousness: Ethical Dimensions and Concerns. AJOB Neuroscience, Volume 14, No. 2, pp. 58–71, 2022. https://doi.org/10.1080/21507740.2022.2148773

[60] D. Gamez, 'The Relationships Between Intelligence and Consciousness in Natural and Artificial Systems,' Journal of Artificial Intelligence and Consciousness, 07:01, pp. 51-62, 2020.

[61] A. I. Shevchenko, M. S. Klymenko, 'Developing a Model of Artificial Conscience', 15th IEEE Int. Conference on Computer Sciences and Information Technologies, CSIT'2020, Vol. 1, 23-26 September 2020, Lviv-Zbarazh, pp. 51–54, 2020. DOI:10.1109/CSIT49958.2020.93219 62

[62] V. Slyusar, et al., 'Some Aspects of Artificial Intelligence Development Strategy for Mobile Technologies,' Journal of Mobile Multimedia, Vol. 20, Iss. 03, 2024, pp. 525–554. https://doi.org/10.13052/jmm1550-464 6.2031

[63] Y. Kondratenko, et al., 'Towards Implementing the Strategy of Artificial Intelligence Development: Ukraine Peculiarities', CEUR Workshop Proceedings, vol. 3513, 2023, pp. 106-117, https://ceur-ws.org/Vol-35 13/paper09.pdf

[64] A. Vaswani, et al., 'Attention is all you need. In Advances in neural information processing systems,' pp. 5998-6008, 2017. https://doi.org/ 10.48550/arXiv.1706.03762

[65] V.I. Slyusar, 'A family of face products of matrices and its properties,' Cybernetics and Systems Analysis, 35 (3), pp. 379–384, 1999. DOI: 10.1007/BF02733426

[66] V.I. Slyusar, 'End matrix products in radar applications,' Izvestiya VUZ: Radioelektronika, 41 (3), pp. 71–75, 1998.

[67] V.I. Slyusar, 'New operations of matrix products for application of radars,' IEEE MTT/ED/AP West Ukraine Chapter DIPED 1997 - Direct and Inverse Problems of Electromagnetic and Acoustic Theory, art. no. 710918, pp. 73 – 74, 1997. DOI: 10.1109/DIPED.1997.710918

[68] V.I. Slyusar, 'Application of Neural Network Technologies for Underwater Munitions Detection,' Radioelectronics and Communications Systems, 65 (12), pp. 654–664, 2022. DOI:10.3103/S07352727230 30020

[69] 'Artificial intelligence now has a "conscience",' 2023. https://portaltele .com.ua/news/technology/u-shtuchnogo-intelektu-teper-ye-sovist.html

[70] O. Striuk, et al., 'Generative Adversarial Neural Networks and Deep Learning: Successful Cases and Advanced Approaches', International Journal of Computing, Vol. 20, Issue 3, pp. 339-349, 2021. https://doi.org/10.47839/ijc.20.3.2278

[71] R. Duro, et al. (eds), 'Advances in Intelligent Robotics and Collaborative Automation', River Publishers, Aalborg, 2015. https://doi.org/10.13052/rp-9788793237049

[72] A.N. Tkachenko, et al., 'Evolutionary adaptation of control processes in robots operating in non-stationary environments', Mechanism and Machine Theory, Vol. 18, No. 4, pp. 275-278, 1983. DOI:10.1016/0094-114X(83)90118-0

[73] Y. P. Kondratenko, O. V. Kozlov, O. S. Gerasin, et al., 'Synthesis and research of neuro-fuzzy observer of clamping force for mobile robot automatic control system,' 2016 IEEE First International Conference on Data Stream Mining & Processing (DSMP), Lviv, Ukraine, 2016, pp. 90-95. DOI: 10.1109/DSMP.2016.7583514

[74] Y. P. Kondratenko, 'Robotics, Automation and Information Systems: Future Perspectives and Correlation with Culture, Sport and Life Science. In: A. Gil-Lafuente, C. Zopounidis (eds) Decision Making and Knowledge Decisio n Support Systems, Lecture Notes in Economics and Mathematical Systems, Vol. 675, Springer, Cham, pp. 43-55, 2015. https://doi.org/10.1007/978-3-319-03907-7_6

6

From Machine Learning to Human Learning: What Can Pedagogy Learn from AI Successes

Victor Timchenko[1], Yuriy Kondratenko[2,3] Olga Kosheleva[4], and Vladik Kreinovich[5]

[1]Admiral Makarov National University of Shipbuilding, Ukraine
[2]Petro Mohyla Black Sea National University, Ukraine
[3]Institute of Artificial Intelligence Problems, Ukraine
[4]Department of Teacher Education, University of Texas at El Paso, USA
[5]Department of Computer Science, University of Texas at El Paso, USA
E-mail: vl.timchenko58@gmail.com; y_kondrat2002@yahoo.com; olgak@utep.edu; vladik@utep.edu

Abstract

Many machine learning techniques – including many techniques behind the current AI-based boom in machine learning – come from the analysis of successful human learning strategies (and researchers expect that other human learning experiences can lead to even more effective AI-based systems). At this moment, so much experience have been accumulated in AI-based machine learning that it is time to start the analysis in the opposite direction – to see what can human-based pedagogy learn from AI successes. In this chapter, we provide the first results of such an analysis – some of which go somewhat against the current pedagogical wisdom.

6.1 Machine Learning and Human Learning – Past, Present, and Future: A Brief Introduction

Machine learning and human learning: recent past. Human learning is as old as humanity itself: we all learn from our parents, from our teachers, from

DOI: 10.1201/9788743809258-6

our mentors. During thousands of years, humanity have accumulated a lot of experience in teaching and learning:

- we know what works and why;
- we know what does not work so well and why.

For many thousands of years, learning has been done by human teachers. When computers were invented, machines capable of what before considered intellectual functions, a natural idea was to help computers learn, i.e., to start the discipline of machine learning [1].

How did researchers come up with ideas? One of the main ideas was to look for how we humans learn – just like if you want to create a flying machine, a natural idea is to look at creatures that fly – e.g., birds. And indeed, many machine learning techniques came from how we learn:

- from neural networks that emulate our learning on the neuron level
- to techniques emulating learning on higher level.

Already on this stage:

- there were some successes in machine learning that overdid human doing similar learning tasks,
- but still, in comparison with thousands of years of successful human learning, the number of these machine learning successes was very small.

So still, the main progress in human learning was largely based only on human-learning experience.

Machine learning and human learning: present. With the development of deep learning, the situation is starting to change. Every day, newer and newer examples appear when machine learning systems provide better results that trained humans – be it:

- in many areas of medical diagnostics or
- in search for new molecules.

see, e.g., [2].

- While the number of successes of human learning continues to grow relatively slow – at approximately the same pace as in the past,
- the number of successes of machine learning is growing exponentially.

Already the number of machine learning successes has grown so fast that it is comparable to the number of human learning successes – and soon, it will overcome that number. This leads us to the next stage.

Machine learning and human learning – future: we need to use the experience of machine learning to come up with better human learning. To get better learning strategies, we learn from the past learning experiences:

- we learn to use techniques that turned out to be effective, and
- we learn not to use techniques that were not effective.

In the past, as we have mentioned, most such experiences came from human learning. However, nowadays:

- as majority of learning success stories come from machine learning, and
- as the proportion of machine learning successes becomes closer and closer to 1,
- it is important to learn from successes and failures of machine learning.

This is, of course, already done when our main purpose is to develop better machine learning tools. However, it is also reasonable to use the machine learning experience to develop better human learning strategies. This brings up to the main purpose of this paper.

What we do in this chapter. In this chapter, we describe how the main features of successful machine learning can be used to help human learning. We present our conclusions in several sections of this chapter, sections corresponding to different aspects of human learning.

It should be mentioned that somewhat unexpectedly, we come up with several conclusions that seems to contradict the usual pedagogical wisdom.

6.2 Who Can Learn?

What is the question? Before we start planning education strategies, it is important to decide whether each of the planned students is able to master this material.

What experience of human pedagogy teaches us. Experience of human pedagogy seems to indicate that some topics are not for everyone. For example:

- everyone can learn the high school physics, but
- not everyone can successfully pass PhD-level classes in theoretical physics.

Similarly:

- everyone can learn to play piano and to sing more or less in tune, but
- not everyone can successfully pass graduate-level music performance classes to become a skilled performer.

It is worth mentioning that even the idea that everyone can master high school subjects (such as basic math) is reasonably new. Even in the 19th century, many people believed that women and people of lower social status are unable to master these subjects – and many US folks still believe that, e.g., to master Calculus, one needs to have a specially organized brain. Such beliefs are not common in Europe, where dozens of years of required high school education has shown that indeed, people are capable of learning all this.

However, most people – and most researchers in pedagogy – do believe that a special brain is needed to become a theoretical physicists or a performing musician.

Comment. Not both, by the way:

- while Albert Einstein was clearly a genius in physics,
- his ability to play violin was always on an amateur level.

Several memoirs of young physicists of his time mention that before their introduction to Einstein, they were warned that:

- while Einstein loves constructive criticisms of his physical ideas,
- he is really hurt when someone criticizes his violin skills.

But what can we learn about it from the current AI success? A human being is born with a largely preorganized network of neurons, a network that allows a newborn baby to cry, to feed, even to swim if placed in water.

- Some brains have more neurons and/or are better organized by the birth time.
- Some brains have fewer neurons and/or are not as well organized.

However, all these brains have the same basic structure – that later becomes more and more developed as the baby learns.

In contrast, the current AI successes:

- do not come from the specially organized neural network with predetermined weights;
- they come from a neural network in which initial weights are assigned randomly.

From this viewpoint, the starting state of AI learning is not even the state of the newborn baby. We could call it the state of the amoeba except that the starting neural network has much more neurons than an amoeba.

And still, starting from this very primitive state, the AI systems manage to learn many skills that, for humans, require an equivalent to a PhD – such as the ability to reliably diagnose rare diseases.

What this shows is that to learn such complex topics, there is no need to have a specially structured brain – so *anyone can learn* all the courses needed to get a PhD in mathematics or in theoretical physics and become a professional in these disciplines.

Of course, like with every other topic:

- some people will learn this material faster, while
- others will require more time to learn this material,

but eventually, everyone will learn.

6.3 In What Order Should We Teach?

How this is usually done. When we want students to learn a lot of material – that does not fit into a single class – then we divide this material into classes:

- first, we teach the basics;
- then, we teach more complex stuff; and
- finally, we teach the most complex technical details.

What can be learn about it from the AI successes? The current AI successes are obtained by using *deep learning*, where all the layers of the neural network learn at the same time.

- Researchers tried to train one layer at a time.
- However, training all the layers at the same time turned out to be much more effective.

In a deep neural network, roughly speaking:

- the first layer corresponds to facts;
- the next layer corresponds to more general notions;
- and, in general, each following layer corresponds to the next level of abstraction.

From this viewpoint, learning all the layers at the same time means that we should learn the whole materials in each course. For example:

- instead of studying the basics of programming in Computer Science I course;

- we should study all the levels of programming in this course; and
- then refine our knowledge of all the levels in each following course.

There is another AI-based reason why this learning scheme would work the best. Namely, in AI, it is often very effective to do what is called *transfer learning*: instead of starting from scratch, we start with a network training for one task, and re-train it for another task. This way, instead of first studying one topic from scratch and then another topic from scratch, we use whatever we learned in the first topic to start learning the second topic as well.

This is somewhat similar to how students are taught in high school, but for most higher education courses, this is a radical idea. It has a potential advantage. For example, now engineering students first study calculus – often without a clear idea of why this is needed in engineering. Because of this lack of understanding, they often do not take this course seriously enough – and thus, at the next semester, when they take an engineering course in which calculus is used, they need to re-learn calculus. In the above-described AI-motivated arrangement, the students study both calculus and its applications at about the same time. Thus, they better understand the need for calculus and hence, waste less time on re-learning it.

6.4 Related Question: Do We Need Rigorous Foundations?

How this is done now. As we have mentioned in the previous section, many science and engineering courses – especially physics courses – are based on mathematical foundations: mostly on calculus and differential equations. These foundational courses are usually taught by mathematics faculty, who try their best to present this material in a rigorous way – the way of mathematics.

Many engineers and physicists believe that for their students, most of this rigor is a waste of time, all the students need is to remember the techniques, and there is no need for them to learn the foundations of these techniques. There have been less-rigorous textbooks written by such engineers and scientists [9] but these textbooks are an exception.

What can we learn about this from AI successes? It is known that modern AI systems are not good in reasoning and in rigor – but nevertheless, they produce much better results than systems based on rigorous derivations.

From this viewpoint, to make teaching of physicists and engineers more effective, it makes sense to decrease the amount of rigor in foundational classes to the bare minimum.

6.5 How Should We Teach: Special Learning Techniques Can Be Helpful, but Is It Possible to Learn Without Them?

What modern pedagogy teaches us. Many pedagogical publications start with the fact that there are some problems with students learning required material. Then these papers:

- describe new teaching techniques – be it active learning, using group-work, etc; and
- show that the use of these techniques leads to a statistically significant improvement of the learning results.

This creates an impression that learning success is not possible if we only use traditional learning tools. This impression is rarely stated explicitly, but implicitly it is there: no one proposes a new method that would simply allow, e.g., 8th grade students to learn the material twice faster.

But what can we learn about it from AI successes? Interestingly, AI successes *do not* come from any sophisticated learning techniques: they are based on the simplest possible optimization technique – gradient descent. This technique used to be described in courses on Numerical Mathematics as an example of a technique that is not recommended due to its simplicity – but AI successes brought this technique's revival. Moreover, attempts to use more complex learning techniques led to worse results – that is why gradient descent is still actively used.

What this seems to indicate, in regard to human education, is that, in principle, we can learn even the most complex subjects by using only the traditional teaching techniques. This does not mean that more complex techniques are not helpful: they can make learning faster and more reliable – but in principle, contrary to the impression that one gets from reading the modern pedagogical papers, we can learn everything by using only these techniques.

6.6 How Do We Teach: Is There a Need to Drill on Many Examples?

How this was done in the past and what pedagogy teaches us. In the past, students would have to do a lot of similar exercises on each topic. Such a drill approach is still practiced, but many pedagogical papers prefer more creative solutions.

What can we learn about this from AI successes? AI successes are largely based on training on thousands of similar examples – exactly what drill is about.

From this viewpoint, it looks like drill should remain an important part of teaching. It is definitely a good idea to make this drill less boring by adding some creativity, but it looks like drill should remain.

6.7 Need to Balance Positive and Negative Examples

How this is usually done. In traditional learning, students are mostly trained on correct solutions – this is what is typically explained in class, sometimes with a few examples of typical mistakes.

What can we learn about this from AI successes? The experience of AI is that learning works the best where we have approximately the same number of positive and negative examples.

With respect to human learning, this means that we need to provide students not only with many correct examples, we also need to provide them with as many incorrect examples, examples on which students will need to learn how to avoid the corresponding mistakes.

This seems to be a completely new idea in pedagogy. It is desirable to try it. Our hope is that it will work, since this is related to the known problem of partial credit. Let us illustrate this problem on the following simplified example. Suppose that we give a test with 10 problems, each worth 10 points. To solve each problem, the student needs to correctly perform 10 steps – and usually, instructors give 1 point for correctly performing each step. If for each of 10 problems, the student performs correctly 9 out of 10 steps, this student gets 9 points for each of these problems. So, this student's overall grade is $10 \cdot 9 = 90$, which is still A ("excellent"). So:

- by accommodating partial credit, the student gets an excellent grade on the 10-problem test, while
- in all 10 problems, the student's answers are wrong.

Hopefully, students who are more exposed to possible mistakes will be more careful and avoid such a situation.

6.8 Possibility of Visualization

How this is done now. Of course, everyone understands that visualization is helpful. In some topics, there are good visualization techniques, while in many others, there are none. It is not even clear whether a good visualization is possible for some abstract topics.

What can we learn about this from AI successes? One of the main reasons why some things are difficult to visualize is that:

- in many problems, we perform computations with high accuracy, but
- in visualization, we can only achieve a certain level of accuracy – e.g., we can only distinguish a small number of intensity levels, as small number of colors, etc.

At first glance, this may seem like a serious obstacle to visualization. However, in AI-based machine learning, there are empirical results – that are justified by a rigorous mathematical analysis – showing that for training, it is enough to use 8-bit numbers [4], i.e., numbers that have only $2^8 = 256$ distinguishable values.

This number is exactly how many colors we can distinguish – which shows that we can always use colors to describe all intermediate stages of the desired computations. In other words, visualization is always possible.

This can be also used to speed up computations. It is worth mentioning that not only visualization is always possible, but we can also use the color interpretation of numbers, and process color signals instead of computer-based real numbers [3, 5, 7, 8]:

- this is faster – since colored light travels with the speed of light – the largest physically possible speed, and
- several light beams can be easily processed in parallel, thus further speeding up the computation process.

6.9 How to Assess Learning and How to Motivate Students?

How learning is assessed now, and what modern pedagogy teaches us about it. Once the teaching is over, we need to assess how well the students learned. Traditionally, the student's level of knowledge is accessed by comparing the student's answers with the correct answers:

- if all the student's answers are correct, the student gets a higher grade, while
- otherwise, if some answers are wrong, the student's grade is lower.

Many modern pedagogical publications propose to change the traditional ways of assessment. Some researchers propose not to grade students' work at all – at least for some material. Other researchers propose to replace the overall grade for a test and/or for a class with a list of grades describing the student's level of knowledge in different categories.

Some publications show that these assessment changes lead to more effective learning. On the other hand, the experience of some of our colleagues – who have tried to implement these ideas – has shown that students are often confused by these changes.

What can we learn about this from AI successes? For training, all AI systems use simple objective functions that are based on similarity between the desired answers and the answers provided by the system on the current stage of training. Attempts to introduce more complex assessment techniques did not lead to more effective AI training.

From this viewpoint, it looks like the traditional assessment techniques are good enough for training. The only change may be that:

- while originally, neural networks used the least squares optimization function – that is known to lead to the final grade being a linear combination of individual grades [6];
- modern AI systems use non-quadratic objective functions, that result in non-linear combination of individual grades.

From this viewpoint, it may be beneficial to explore nonlinear techniques for combining grades for individual assignments into a single grade.

Acknowledgments

This work was supported in part by the National Science Foundation grants 1623190 (A Model of Change for Preparing a New Generation for Professional Practice in Computer Science), HRD-1834620 and HRD-2034030 (CAHSI Includes), EAR-2225395 (Center for Collective Impact in Earthquake Science C-CIES), and by the AT&T Fellowship in Information Technology.

It was also supported by a grant from the Hungarian National Research, Development and Innovation Office (NRDI), and by the Institute for Risk and Reliability, Leibniz Universitaet Hannover, Germany.

References

[1] C. M. Bishop, Pattern Recognition and Machine Learning, Springer, New York, 2006.

[2] I. Goodfellow, Y. Bengio, A. Courville, 'Deep Learning', MIT Press, Cambridge, Massachusetts, 2016.

[3] O. Kosheleva, V. Kreinovich, V. L. Timchenko, Y. P. Kondratenko, 'From Fuzzy to Mobile Fuzzy', Journal of Mobile Multimedia, Vol. 20, No. 3, 2024, pp. 651-664. https://doi.org/10.13052/jmm1550-4646.2035

[4] C. Q. Lauter, A. Volkova, 'A framework for semi-automatic precision and accuracy analysis for fast and rigorous deep learning', in: M. Cornea, W. Liu, A. Tisserand (Eds) Proceedings of the 27th IEEE Symposium on Computer Arithmetic ARITH 2020, Portland, Oregon, June 7-10, 2020, pp. 103-110.

[5] A. Lupo, O. Kosheleva, V. Kreinovich, V. Timchenko, and Y. Kondratenko, 'There is still plenty of room at the bottom: Feynman's vision of quantum computing 65 years later', in: Y. P. Kondratenko and A. I. Shevchenko (Eds) Research Tendencies and Prospect Domains for AI Development and Implementation, River Publishers, Denmark, 2024, pp. 77-86. DOI:10.1201/9788770046947-4

[6] D. J. Sheskin, 'Handbook of Parametric and Nonparametric Statistical Procedures', Chapman and Hall/CRC, Boca Raton, Florida, 2011.

[7] V. Timchenko, Y. Kondratenko, V. Kreinovich, 'Logical Platforms for Mobile Application in Decision Support Systems Based on Color Information Processing', Journal of Mobile Multimedia, Vol. 20, No. 3, 2024, pp. 679-698. https://doi.org/10.13052/jmm1550-4646.2037

[8] V. Timchenko, V. Kreinovich, Y. Kondratenko, V. Horbov, 'Effectiveness Evaluations of Optical Color Fuzzy Computing', in: Y. P. Kondratenko, A. I. Shevchenko (Eds) Research Tendencies and Prospect Domains for AI Development and Implementation, River Publishers, Denmark, 2024, pp. 129-151. DOI:10.1201/9788770046947-7

[9] Ya. B. Zel'dovich, I. M. Yaglom, 'Higher Math for Beginners', Prentice Hall, Hoboken, New Jersey, 1988.

7

Perspectives of AI Applications for Improving Learning and Teaching Processes

V. I. Slyusar

Institute of Artificial Intelligence Problems, Ukraine
E-mail: swadim@ukr.net

Abstract

The chapter presents the concept of an ecosystem of neuro-coworkers within an educational institution as an innovative approach to integrating large language models (LLMs) into the processes of learning, teaching, and administrative management. It introduces a concept of a multi-agent architecture that envisions the interaction of various types of neuro-coworkers forming a unified cognitive system of the institution. The prospects of establishing inter-university networks that facilitate knowledge exchange among educational institutions through a centralized system of federated model training are examined. Approaches are proposed to address the issues of function duplication and inconsistency among neuro-coworkers by implementing a unified cognitive core with enhanced capabilities for personalizing the educational process. The use of 3D world generation technologies is discussed as a means for visualizing educational material and applying knowledge in practice, particularly in literature, physics, and mathematics. Special attention is given to the role of artificial general intelligence (AGI) in the formation of superknowledge and the transformation of the educational process at the level of researcher training, with a forecasted paradigm shift in the interaction between human intelligence and AI. The necessity of developing cognitive

DOI: 10.1201/9788743809258-7

assistants for interpreting and integrating knowledge generated by AI is substantiated, along with the need to design symbiotic learning systems for the effective utilization of AGI capabilities in future scientific and educational environments.

Keywords: Large Language Model, AI, Virtual Reality, AGI, SI.

7.1 Introduction

LLMs have significant potential for application in the educational and academic-pedagogical domains [1–3]. Drawing on practical experience with ChatGPT, GPT-4 [4–8], o1 [9, 10], o3-mini, the Gemini family of LLMs [11], DeepSeek [12, 13], and other language models [14–21], it is possible to outline potential directions for deploying artificial intelligence (AI) platforms based on LLMs in teaching, learning, and research processes. First and foremost, it should be emphasized that GPT-4 and its more advanced successors can effectively function as personal instructors, providing information across diverse domains and explaining concepts to help pupils or students gain a better understanding of educational material [22–25]. AI-based platforms are capable of creating more personalized and adaptive learning environments for remote education. Such technologies facilitate access to education for individuals residing in remote areas or those with special needs by converting text into speech for visually impaired students or offering simplified explanations for individuals with cognitive impairments. LLMs such as GPT-4o can be used continuously to engage in dialogue with students, generate responses to their queries, and even conduct seminars and discussions, allowing learners to study according to their own schedules and at their own pace. In essence, these LLMs serve as powerful tools for personalized education, offering valuable experiences for targeted development of knowledge, skills, and competencies by adapting to each learner's individual needs. LLMs are capable of assessing a learner's current level of understanding and providing specialized content and exercises to support improvement. In effect, this enables the large-scale deployment of neuro-pedagogical staff delivering fundamental educational services, responding to student inquiries via Telegram bots and websites, including through voice-supported interfaces. The relevant approaches will be examined in more detail below.

7.2 Ecosystem of neuro-coworkers in educational institutions

Modern educational institutions are faced with the necessity of adapting the learning process to the rapid advancement of AI technologies.

Conception of the university's neuro-ecosystem. The concept of neuro-coworkers is grounded in the use of intelligent agents powered by GPT-4 or another LLMs, which offer extensive support capabilities for instructors, students, and administrative staff. This transformation of the educational process is implemented through the comprehensive deployment of a hierarchical system of neuro-coworkers that perform various functions within the educational environment. The key components of such an ecosystem include:

1. Neuro-consultant – a virtual assistant focused on providing responses related to internal documents, regulations, and platform-specific instructions. This enables both institutional staff and students to quickly access the necessary information, thereby optimizing internal communication within the university.
2. Neuro-curator – an intelligent agent offering 24/7 support to students. Integrated into chatbots and educational platforms, it enables students to receive accurate and timely responses to academic and administrative questions.
3. Neuro-tutor and neuro-examiner – tools designed for personalized learning and automated knowledge assessment. The neuro-tutor provides interactive assistance during lessons, while the neuro-examiner conducts testing and evaluates submitted assignments.
4. Neuro-lecturer – a new component of the educational process that complements or replaces traditional instructors. It delivers lectures automatically, analyzes student comprehension, and adapts content accordingly. It answers questions in real time using knowledge bases, course materials, and past session context. The neuro-lecturer integrates into online and traditional courses, supplementing face-to-face learning or replacing it in remote formats.
5. Neuro-tech support – an automated system for processing inquiries from students and faculty, capable of resolving up to 60% of requests without human intervention. This reduces the administrative burden and improves the quality of support services.

6. Neuro-HR – an intelligent career counseling system that helps students prepare résumés, assess professional competencies, and identify suitable job opportunities after graduation.

It should be emphasized that the implementation of the neuro-coworker concept in the educational process represents a promising direction for the transformation of all areas of education. Intelligent agents are capable of performing essential support and instructional functions, reducing the workload on educators while enhancing the personalization of the learning process. The neuro-lecturer opens new opportunities for the flexible adaptation of lecture content, making the educational experience more interactive and effective. This approach demonstrates substantial potential for the further advancement of educational technologies and can be scaled to encompass the entire spectrum of educational activities.

The list of typical neuro-coworkers within educational institutions can be expanded by introducing an LLM-based neuro-methodologist, whose task is to develop or update existing lecture materials and coursework. Another valuable addition could be the integration of a neuro-psychologist service [26] into the educational process, which would support student motivation and address mental health challenges. Within the framework of such psychological assistance, AI should be considered an effective tool for providing emotional support, helping learners cope with stress and maintain mental balance. This may include mindfulness exercises, stress management techniques, or simply offering compassionate interaction. An intelligent chatbot [26] can help detect situations in which a student is experiencing emotional difficulties and suggest appropriate resources or interventions. In this context, AI can serve as a personal assistant that guides students through their studies, offering advice on course selection, or even personal development.

The most suitable platforms for the proposed implementation of AI are distance learning systems, particularly in the fields of information technology (IT) and programming. However, provided that the educational process is sufficiently digitalized, the concept of neuro-pedagogical personnel can gradually be introduced into traditional educational institutions as well. For example, such an experiment was announced in 2024 at David Game College (United Kingdom) [27].

It is important to note that the implementation of this approach should be accompanied by a comprehensive set of measures to eliminate the fragmentation of neuro-coworkers, which often results in functional overlap, reduced interaction efficiency among different systems, and increased complexity in system management. To address this issue, it is necessary to develop a unified ecosystem of neuro-coworkers, integrated into the digital infrastructure of the educational institution, that enables coordinated interaction among all intelligent agents.

The concept of a typical neuro-coworker ecosystem within an educational institution involves the use of a unified architectural framework, based on the creation of a core cognitive layer that integrates all representatives of the neuro-staff. This core operates on a multi-agent basis, whereby the set of minimally required agents must ensure the following:

- Shared access to knowledge through a unified knowledge base, accessible to all neuro-agents, which helps avoid inconsistencies in responses and prevents information redundancy.
- The presence of a modular interface through which different neuro-coworkers (such as the neuro-lecturer, neuro-curator, neuro-tutor, etc.) are interconnected via a unified API-based access system, ensuring their seamless interaction.
- Centralized analytics with a unified monitoring system for the performance of all neuro-coworkers, enabling the analysis and evaluation of their efficiency, identification of bottlenecks, and improvement of the overall user experience.

Intelligent interaction among all agents within the ecosystem presupposes that neuro-coworkers exchange information in real time. For instance, if a student poses a question to the neuro-curator but the response requires a more in-depth explanation, the request is automatically redirected to the neuro-lecturer. In responding to student inquiries, the system must consider the student's level of preparation, completed courses, and prior interactions with the system. This enables contextual adaptation of the educational process with personalized learning, allowing the system to generate individual learning trajectories through students' interactions with various neuro-coworkers within the institution.

Additionally, based on data from the neuro-tutor and neuro-examiner, intelligent midterm assessments can be developed and dynamically adjusted according to each student's knowledge and gaps. In the future, this will make it possible to create digital twins of learners [28] for virtually testing all aspects of instructional load adaptation and optimizing teaching methods.

The centralized management and cross-platform compatibility of the proposed ecosystem will allow for the implementation of a unified access layer to the functionality of neuro-coworkers via mobile and web applications with intuitive interfaces. Furthermore, centralization will enable the integration of external services funded by the educational institution – such as cloud-based storage platforms, video conferencing systems, and VR/AR-based learning technologies. An important example of an external service for creating neuro-lecturers is the use of platforms such as A2E [29] and HeyGen [30], which generate AI-based avatar videos. A2E enables the creation of personalized avatars from video footage or photographs of real individuals, accurately reproducing voice, facial expressions, and lip movements. It also offers features such as face replacement, text removal from videos, and video generation from a single image. HeyGen initially provided only standard avatars and exhibited less precise synchronization, although it has improved over time. The choice between these services depends on specific needs: A2E is preferable for personalized content at an affordable cost, while HeyGen is more suitable for rapid creation of standard video content.

In any case, users should be able to interact easily with the avatar system, select the desired neuro-coworker, and receive comprehensive responses. Among the advantages of avatar technologies is the creation of a sense of trust between learners and the neuro-lecturer or other neuro-coworkers, combining cognitive interaction with the benefits of visual communication.

Inter-university cooperation in consolidated neuro-ecosystem. The overall ecosystem can be expanded by integrating new neuro-coworkers and training them to perform updated functions. As a result, an intelligent and adaptive educational environment will be created, enhancing the efficiency of the learning process and the quality of education.

Another direction for scaling involves the integration of neuro-coworker ecosystems across multiple educational institutions. This would enable the formation of a global neural network, uniting educational institutions within a single cognitive environment. Let us consider the corresponding architecture at the inter-university level. A key feature of this structure is the presence of a centralized management layer within the distributed ecosystem of neuro-coworkers. This coordination meta-layer at the top of the ecosystem ensures standardization, data exchange, and optimized interaction among neuro-coworkers from different institutions. It includes: a global knowledge base (a consolidated repository of educational data), protocols for interaction among neuro-coworkers from different universities, and security and access control mechanisms (user identification and differentiation of access levels to information). At the same time, each university operates its own AI system, integrated with the global network. These local educational ecosystems of neuro-coworkers serve the students and faculty of the respective institution, are adapted to internal academic programs, and exchange data with the global network as needed.

Interaction among neuro-coworkers from different universities is based on a hybrid principle. This approach enables decentralized knowledge exchange, allowing neuro-coworkers from local institutions to directly access the global knowledge base or consult neuro-coworkers from other institutions. For instance, if one university develops a new educational module, it can be uploaded to the global system and made available for use by other institutions. In this way, faculty and students can access specialized materials from other universities through secure communication and data exchange channels.

The main mechanisms of inter-university interaction at the level of the consolidated knowledge base assume that each educational institution contributes unique educational content or develops it collaboratively with other interested parties. Neuro-coworkers across universities can exchange materials via an intelligent search system using a trusted source mechanism, which prevents the dissemination of inaccurate information. Through this framework, universities can select virtual lecturers who deliver courses to students from multiple institutions, thereby establishing a shared pool of inter-university neuro-lecturers. The system automatically translates lectures into various languages and adapts the material to the specific audience. Different neuro-lecturers may also interact with one another, clarifying course details or directing students to highly specialized resources.

If a student from one university encounters difficulties, they can consult a neuro-tutor from another institution that specializes in the relevant subject area. This is particularly beneficial for interdisciplinary programs and international projects, where the required knowledge may extend beyond the scope of a single institution.

In addition to neuro-lecturers, neuro-curators and tutors will also operate at the inter-university level. These agents will engage in self-learning across a broader student audience, synthesizing best practices and pedagogical approaches. In turn, neuro-examiners from different universities can synchronize their standards, contributing to the creation of unified assessment criteria. The inter-university neuro-system will enable automated testing of students from different countries based on shared principles for collective examination and certification. To support graduates in finding employment within international academic and industrial projects, an inter-university HR system will be established. In this network, neuro-HR agents from various institutions can exchange information about job vacancies, internships, and grants, as well as foster collaboration between universities and companies [31]. To ensure the effective functioning of the proposed inter-university ecosystem, it is necessary to implement the following: consolidated machine learning with the exchange of trained LLMs; unified API access to enable communication between universities as a standard interface for interaction among neuro-coworkers from different institutions; blockchain verification to protect educational data and track the authenticity of academic achievements; adaptive AI models to allow each neural system to tailor shared knowledge to its local context. The formation of a global educational environment in this manner will provide students and faculty with access to unique educational materials from a wide range of institutions, including their library and archival collections.

Institutions of higher education will be able to jointly develop innovative academic programs and unified testing systems to enhance the objectivity of knowledge assessment. Particular attention should be given to the emergence of new opportunities for inter-university collaboration in the scientific domain, supported by interdisciplinary datasets from various academic fields. Collaborative training of neural systems based on combined data will lead to the creation of universal models that more effectively support interdisciplinary research. Therefore, it is already advisable to intensify efforts to digitize existing scientific publications and university historical archives, in order to expand the volume of datasets available for continued training of language models.

In conclusion, the formation of a global ecosystem of neuro-coworkers for collaboration among educational institutions will enable the synchronization of educational processes across universities, enhance knowledge accessibility for students worldwide, and optimize inter-university interaction through intelligent knowledge exchange systems. Collectively, these developments will foster the creation of a universal educational environment where learning becomes truly personalized, accessible, and technologically advanced. The concept described herein may serve as the foundation for a new era of digital education, in which AI plays a pivotal role in the global exchange of knowledge.

AI-assistance for teachers and students. In addition to neuro-coworkers who partially or fully perform the functions of teaching staff, virtual teaching assistants should also be regarded as an important component of the proposed ecosystem. Just as AI can support students, it is equally capable of assisting educators by providing feedback on their performance, identifying areas where individual teachers may experience challenges, and offering additional support. AI can recommend professional development resources to educators, such as strategies for improving teaching methods or updates on the latest research in their field.

By utilizing LLMs such as GPT-4o, educators can automate certain aspects of the teaching process. For instance, LLMs can automatically assess assignments or generate instructional content, including lecture summaries, self-assessment questions, interactive practice exercises, quizzes, lesson plans, examples, and scenarios to illustrate complex topics. AI can also serve as an auxiliary tool during the peer review process by detecting potential issues in manuscript drafts, such as plagiarism or deviations from grammatical and punctuation norms, and by offering suggestions to improve clarity and coherence.

Another area of application is the effective management of institutional resources using local LLMs. These models can support optimal distribution of teaching workloads, class scheduling, library resource management, coordination of student services, and summarization of academic performance at the departmental or institutional level based on semester or annual results. A pressing task is to lay the groundwork for the future integration of AI technologies into the process of generating compromise solutions in typical administrative scenarios. This approach would allow for the generalization of best management practices and the renewal of conceptual frameworks for their implementation. The aforementioned psychologist chatbot [26] can provide helpful advice and assist in navigating critical situations.

By employing AI as an instructional tool, teachers can train students to identify and analyze the inherent limitations of AI, thereby fostering the development of critical thinking skills. Locally deployed LLMs within educational institutions can facilitate collaborative learning by coordinating group projects, creating environments for discussion, and providing feedback on group dynamics related to knowledge acquisition or task performance. In this context, it is advisable to apply reinforcement learning (RL) methodology [32, 33] to adjust workload volume and timing at the group level.

One of the most valuable capabilities of AI is its ability to generate dynamic simulations or scenarios that allow students to apply their knowledge within a virtual environment [23]. This will be discussed in more detail in the following section. It is also important to highlight the multilingual capabilities of LLMs, which enable the creation of multilingual educational resources and expand global access to education. By providing instant feedback on grammar, pronunciation, and vocabulary, AI serves as a powerful tool for learning both native and foreign languages. It can support conversational practice in a safe, nonjudgmental environment, offer real-time translation services, and thus facilitate learning and collaboration among students who speak different languages.

In 2023, the GPT-4 webpage provided access to various tutoring plugins. Among them were notable tools such as Tutory (on-demand tutoring), Open Lecture (highlighting key moments in open course lectures for focused learning), Giga Tutor (an AI-based tutor that retained personalized answers to questions), edX (which curated courses and content from leading universities to expand user knowledge at any level), and ABCmouse (offering educational activities for children aged 2–8).

Unfortunately, as of January 2024, OpenAI discontinued plugin support in GPT-4 and replaced them with newer functionalities known as tools. These include the web browser for retrieving up-to-date information and accessing external services, a code interpreter for calculations and data analysis, and the DALL-E image generator. According to the developers, this transition was made to optimize performance and improve the integration of new features. Therefore, if a reader is interested in a specific function previously available through plugins, it may now be implemented using the available tools or through the API interface. Nevertheless, some specialized educational functionalities continue to be supported by OpenAI through user-created custom versions of GPT-4, known as GPTs. Examples of such language-tutoring GPTs include "Language Teacher. Ms. Smith" and "Speak AI: English Conversation Practice & Writing." These services are notable for utilizing the voice interface of GPT-4o. In particular, "Language Teacher. Ms. Smith" offers voice-based instruction in 20 languages. For users wishing to study English, the service first assesses their proficiency level (Beginner, Intermediate, or Advanced) and then proposes a list of topics tailored to that level.

A similar tutoring function for mathematics is provided by GPTs such as "Math Solver." Access to these and other specialized GPTs is readily available via the "Explore GPTs" section on the user's personal page in ChatGPT.

7.3 Synthesis of 3D Worlds as an Educational Technology

A promising trend in the educational process is the integration of LLMs with generative transformers capable of synthesizing 2D and 3D images and videos. This opens up vast opportunities for creativity and the enhancement of teaching and learning processes.

Prompts and their AI-driven visualization. Of particular interest is the idea of introducing a lesson on 3D world generation from text or audio descriptions for younger students. This approach holds great potential for developing creative and spatial thinking, as well as skills related to modern IT technologies. Let us examine possible approaches to implementing this concept in more detail.

The primary goal of such lessons is to teach children how to transform their ideas and imagination into 3D environment using audio descriptions as instructions for generating corresponding content. This encourages the development of imagination, creativity, and basic communication skills with generative AI. The lesson format can be structured as follows:

1. In the introductory part, the teacher explains what 3D worlds are and shows examples – simple models created in games or graphical editors.
2. In the main part of the lesson, students are trained to formulate audio descriptions of 3D scenes. Pupils are invited to describe in words the kind of world they wish to create and listen to examples of pre-prepared audio descriptions – either created by the teacher or generated by AI according to the intended 3D concept. In the next step, the generation tools are demonstrated. For instance, using software for 3D content synthesis (such as educational versions of Minecraft, or simpler AI tools), several audio descriptions proposed by students are converted into basic models, which they can later refine at their discretion.
3. In the practical part of the lesson, students work individually or in small groups to edit the generated models, adding details and modifying the 3D world composition. During this phase, the teacher provides assistance and consultation to reinforce the students' newly acquired skills (see Figure 7.1).

To implement the proposed educational technology, the following are required: computers or tablets with installed software; basic VR headsets for viewing the created worlds; and software for generating 3D models from text or audio inputs (for example, algorithms based on GPT-4o or Unity AI Tools).

Closely related to this concept is the AI service developed by World Labs (http://worldlabs.ai/blog), which transforms 2D images into 3D scenes. To use it, students simply need to upload a single image. The neural network then reconstructs the hidden areas and adapts the output to any scene or

Figure 7.1 Teacher's interaction with different student groups during the practical part of the 3D world generation lesson (Ideogram Image Generator).

style. All visual environments are generated in real time, and users can freely navigate through them as in a video game. A representative example is a lesson proposed by GPT-4o:

1. The teacher describes a "mysterious forest" with tall trees, glowing mushrooms emitting a magical light, and a small house in the center. Children listen to the description and imagine what it might look like.
2. The program generates a basic 3D world based on the description.
3. Students add their own elements: for instance, one child creates animals, another adds clouds or a rainbow.

During such lessons, children learn to express their thoughts through new artistic forms, discover the fundamentals of design and modeling, and experience how AI technologies can bring their fantasies and dreams to life in virtual space. This can become a first step toward developing professional interest in fields such as design, architecture, or the gaming industry.

An alternative version of the lesson is also possible, in which the inverse task is solved – determining the prompt used to generate a 3D world. In preparing this type of lesson, the teacher creates a 3D scene in advance, generated from a text prompt, but keeps the content of that prompt secret. The students' task is to reconstruct the original description by observing the nuances of the visual scene in the virtual environment. The lesson may begin with the class divided into groups, each of which is given the opportunity to ask several questions or make a few guesses about the prompt – for example: "Did the description include the word 'castle'?", "Were any characters mentioned?", or "Was a specific historical era referenced?" If a guess is incorrect, the teacher provides a hint – for instance, clarifying that certain objects appeared as a result of a specific detail in the description, or suggesting the general stylistic tone (e.g., fantasy, futuristic, etc.). Gradually, students identify the most important elements that point to key prompt words and attempt to reconstruct the original description. In the final phase, each group formulates its own version of the initial text prompt and identifies the keywords they believe influenced the creation of the world. When the groups present their interpretations, the teacher compares them to the actual prompt, explains how each key word shaped the details of the 3D world, and discusses which phrases or descriptive expressions most significantly influenced the composition and atmosphere of the virtual space.

This approach fosters logical reasoning and inference skills while also cultivating an understanding of how textual descriptions are translated into graphical objects. It adds a gamified element, encouraging students to analyze the relationship between words and visual imagery and to feel like "explorers" uncovering a hidden scenario. Collaboration within these investigative world-building groups also promotes the development of communication skills and teamwork abilities.

Learning "Literature" based on AI. Another direction for applying 3D world generation technology is in literature lessons. This presents a unique opportunity to make the study of classical and contemporary works more engaging and accessible for younger students. Implementing such an idea makes the journey through the world of literature more tangible and relatable to children by visualizing scenes, characters, and the atmosphere of literary works through 3D models. It nurtures imagination, deepens text comprehension, and stimulates interest in reading.

A lesson of this kind can follow several typical stages. While exploring the text, the teacher or students read an excerpt from a book that describes a scene, character, or setting – for example, a forest in a fairy tale or the room of the main character. This is followed by a discussion of the details, during which the teacher asks guiding questions to help students identify the key elements of the description: colors, sizes, surrounding objects, the nature of the character, and so on. Based on the description, children create visual scenes using simple software or a platform that converts text/audio into 3D. After generating the basic scene, students may suggest their own additions, refine the world or its characters (e.g., choose the facial expression of a character, add atmosphere, or adjust lighting). The implementation of this scenario using the example of Cinderella could unfold as follows:

1. The teacher reads a passage describing the ballroom: "Tall white marble columns, a gleaming floor, the lights of chandeliers, golden ornaments on the walls."
2. The children discuss how they imagine the place. The teacher writes down the key descriptive words.
3. The program transforms the description into a 3D scene, and the students add their own details – for example, the placement of guests or a view of the balcony.
4. Similarly, the image of Cinderella is created: "Her dress was as light as a cloud, sky-blue in color, and crystal slippers sparkled on her feet." Students refine or elaborate on the details: the length of the dress, the hairstyle, accessories.

The final prompt for recreating the described scene from Cinderella (Figure 7.2) may be as follows: "A majestic ballroom with tall white marble columns, a polished gleaming floor, and golden ornamental patterns on the walls. The grand chandeliers cast a warm, magical glow, illuminating the royal celebration. The scene is enriched with a soft blue hue, creating a dreamy and enchanting atmosphere. In the center of the scene, a young woman in a flowing, sky-blue gown stands gracefully. Her delicate glass slippers shimmer as they catch the ballroom's light. The overall color palette features cool blue tones, adding a fairy-tale elegance to the composition." The image generated using the specified prompt in Figure 7.2 can subsequently serve as the foundation for constructing a 3D scene using the previously mentioned World Labs service or other similar platforms.

The pedagogical value of such a lesson lies in developing students' ability to deeply understand literary texts. Children learn to read descriptions more attentively and identify essential details in order to create more accurate visualizations. In doing so, they also develop analytical thinking, as they discuss how a character's appearance reflects their personality and how the setting relates to the plot. Visualized scenes help students experience the events of a story more vividly, establishing an emotional connection to the narrative

Figure 7.2 A version of the scene from Cinderella, generated using DALLE-3.

and merging cognitive processes with emotional engagement. As a further development of this approach, it is possible to implement literary analysis courses for high school students or university students, where synthesized 3D scenes are used to explore complex literary topics such as symbolism and metaphor.

Thanks to group projects, where each student group is responsible for synthesizing a specific episode or character in 3D space, a virtual museum of literary works can be created. In addition, based on virtual reality (VR) technologies, students can move through the worlds they have created, which opens up possibilities for implementing the idea of interactive theatres for school performances through VR by generating scenes. To implement multi-character literary scenarios, it is necessary to use multi-agent LLM architectures, where each agent is responsible for reproducing a specific character or for generating dynamic visual scenes. For literature lessons, it is also possible to develop interactive maps in which scenes from a book are combined into a single storyline. Taking Gulliver's Travels as an example, children could create Lilliput, the land of giants, the ship, and other key locations. In each location of such a map, students are given the opportunity to discuss the characters' behavior and events to gain a deeper understanding of the plot. The long-term effect of this approach lies not only in transforming literature lessons into engaging journeys, but also in developing creative skills and stimulating interest in reading, as each student will be able to bring their favorite stories to life.

3D visualization technologies for physical processes for students. For high school students, beyond literature, the integration of 3D world generation technologies is also appropriate in subjects such as physics and mathematics. This approach can become a powerful tool for visualizing complex abstract concepts and transforming them into understandable and imagination-stimulating images. Let us consider how this idea can be implemented in physics lessons. First of all, 3D technologies for visualizing physical processes make it possible to clearly demonstrate phenomena that are difficult for students to imagine. For example, when studying mechanics, the creation of virtual worlds using LLMs allows students to observe Newton's laws in action, collisions of bodies, the operation of levers or pendulums. The teacher can demonstrate the fall of an apple in Earth's gravitational field and then activate a 3D simulation for the Moon. This will allow students to compare the results and, on that basis, derive the law of universal gravitation. To enhance clarity and focus students' attention on key objects in the 3D scenes, their visualization can be complemented by object detection operations [34] or image and video segmentation [35, 36]. Similarly, for better understanding of electricity and magnetism, it is useful to visualize electric circuits, magnetic field lines, or the operation of an electric motor. Likewise, in optics, it is appropriate to demonstrate light reflection and refraction, especially negative refraction characteristic of metamaterials [37], the operation of flat lenses based on this principle, and more.

Such interactive experiments significantly enhance or even replace traditional experiments that require complex equipment. Through virtual investigations, students will be able to observe how physical parameters (mass, velocity, angle, etc.) change as a result of an experiment. 3D models of atoms, molecules, waves, and particles will help students better understand the microworld. For example, the visualization of molecular motion as a function of temperature can support the study of diffusion and thermal conductivity phenomena. The same applies to historical experiments, where virtual reconstructions of famous studies allow students not only to observe them but also to recreate the details of these processes in an interactive format.

3D-visualization in mathematics. In mathematics lessons, 3D geometric visualization technologies are ideally suited for studying solid figures, transformations, and geometric constructions such as the demonstration of complex spatial shapes (polyhedra, ellipsoids, hyperboloids), the development of

3D object nets, the investigation of intersections of solids, or the rotation of figures around an axis. Similarly, spatial visualization of function graphs (especially complex and multidimensional ones) can be performed to better understand their behavior. For instance, it is appropriate to explore graphs of quadratic functions, parabolas, hyperbolas, sinusoids, derivatives, and integrals using 3D methods – with visual representations of areas under curves or tangents. Through 3D modeling, students can also solve practical problems involving trajectory construction, angle and distance calculations, area determination, and volume optimization – for example, identifying the packaging shape that minimizes material use while preserving volume.

An engaging approach is the use of game-based mathematical quests, where students must solve problems in order to progress to the next "level" or unlock a new part of a 3D world. For example, they may need to solve an equation or a system of equations to activate bridges or stairs within the virtual space. Another virtual quest scenario could involve students assisting an architect in constructing a dome. They must calculate the radius, arc lengths, and the optimal angle of inclination for the support beams.

The described virtual worlds transform physics and mathematics from mere "school subjects" and abstract disciplines into exciting "journeys" into the world of science. Visualization allows students to connect abstract concepts to the real world, making learning more personal. Students see how knowledge can be applied to solving real-world problems, fostering interest in fields such as engineering, IT, and other high-tech industries. Different levels of simulation complexity enable teachers to adapt to students' level of preparation and the development of their spatial reasoning, which is especially important in sections of solid geometry, vector, and analytic geometry. For such lessons, in addition to the tools mentioned above, both simple platforms (such as GeoGebra for mathematics and PhET Interactive Simulations for physics) and more advanced 3D modeling and virtual reality environments (such as Blender, Unity, and Unreal Engine) are suitable.

7.4 Large Language Models as a Tool for Acquiring Superknowledge

7.4.1 Superknowledge as a new objective of the educational process in higher education institutions

The concepts of AI usage discussed in the previous sections have encompassed various levels of education – from early primary school to master's programs. At the same time, in the short period since their emergence, LLMs have proven to be valuable tools for supporting researchers and individuals pursuing the educational and scientific level of Doctor of Philosophy. In this context, it should be noted that LLMs are capable of providing rapid access to information, generating text fragments for scientific reports, dissertations, or articles, summarizing large volumes of academic texts, and identifying key themes in the scientific literature. The new rules of the game in this domain are associated with the introduction of OpenAI's Deep Research service and similar offerings by alternative LLM developers and platform integrators (such as perplexity.ai and others).

Machine learning (ML), big data analysis, neural networks, and deep learning algorithms significantly expand the boundaries of understanding complex systems, phenomena, and processes, creating a new cognitive environment for students and educators. LLMs also assist in data analysis and visualization, as well as in performing symbolic computations. In particular, the Wolfram plugin, included in the GPT-4 service in 2023, provided access to powerful mathematical computations, curated knowledge, and real-time data through Wolfram Alpha and Wolfram Language services. Later, with the advent of GPT-4o, these capabilities were transferred to user-customized GPTs.

At the same time, thanks to access to vast amounts of diverse information and the ability to identify non-obvious connections within it, LLMs are enabling a breakthrough in the field of scientific research and development, creating the conditions for the emergence of superknowledge [38], which transforms our understanding of the world and elevates the higher education system to a qualitatively new level. In this context, the acquisition of such knowledge is no longer a matter of science fiction but becomes an integral part of academic reality, reshaping teaching methods, strengthening the role of interdisciplinary approaches, and allowing faster adaptation to the evolving needs of society.

For this reason, an important goal of AI application in higher education, particularly in the training of master's and PhD-level students, should be the pursuit of fundamentally new and previously inaccessible knowledge for humanity [38]. This ambitious objective is linked to the ability of AI to analyze massive volumes of data, detect complex interrelations, and propose solutions that surpass human cognitive capacities. AI is capable of integrating knowledge from multiple disciplines, initiating new research directions, and forecasting trends in scientific development. For example, it can generate hypotheses based on datasets too large or complex for humans to process manually, or identify optimal solutions to intricate problems such as drug discovery, modeling complex economic systems, or analyzing global environmental changes. Let us consider several examples of such superknowledge that have already been acquired with the help of AI.

7.4.2 Examples of Superknowledge Acquisition through Artificial Intelligence

Significant scientific breakthroughs associated with the use of AI are most notably observed in the field of biology. Publication [39] presents the results of applying the multimodal generative language model for biology, ESM3, which is capable of generating novel proteins that differ from known natural analogues. Through parameter scaling, computational power, and vast datasets, ESM3 can simultaneously analyze the sequence, structure, and function of proteins, transforming three-dimensional biological data into discrete alphabets. This opens up new generative possibilities and enables the modeling of evolutionary processes at a superhuman level. ESM3 has demonstrated the ability to create a previously unknown fluorescent protein (esmGFP), the sequence of which shares only 58% similarity with the closest known protein structures. According to researchers, this is equivalent to half a billion years of evolutionary diversification in nature. Through this capability to simulate evolutionary processes, ESM3 stands as an example of superhuman knowledge generated by AI. ESM3 not only reproduces known patterns embedded during its training but also opens new frontiers for programming biology and developing innovative solutions in medicine and biological research.

Another example is the Evo 2 LLM developed by specialists at Arc Institute and NVIDIA [40], which is built on the principles of language modeling but specialized in the analysis and generation of genomic sequences. Evo 2 was trained on 9.3 trillion DNA nucleotides from a carefully curated genomic atlas representing all domains of life. It is capable of predicting the functional impact of genetic variants without additional fine-tuning. The model is available in two versions, with 7 and 40 billion parameters, and features a context window of up to 1 million tokens with single-nucleotide resolution, allowing it to accurately assess the effects of mutations on proteins, RNA, and organism viability. Evo 2 demonstrates high accuracy in predicting the pathogenicity of both coding and non-coding variants, including splice sites and complex mutations. Moreover, analysis of the model's mechanisms revealed that Evo 2 autonomously learns to recognize biologically significant features, such as exon-intron boundaries, transcription factor binding sites, elements of protein secondary structure, and mobile genetic elements. This opens up new possibilities for genome annotation, including for extinct species. Evo 2 is also capable of generating realistic genomic sequences, from mitochondrial genomes to minimal prokaryotic and eukaryotic chromosomes, with guided search during inference, enabling the generation of complex epigenomic patterns and even encoding messages by altering chromatin accessibility. All resources, including model parameters, training and inference code, as well as the OpenGenome2 dataset, are available in open access, allowing for the use and further development of Evo 2's capabilities for deeper understanding and design of biological systems.

Somewhat less fundamental, yet no less impressive, are the achievements demonstrated by the Ithaca project [41] – a system based on deep neural networks designed to restore damaged ancient Greek inscriptions and determine their original location and date of composition. By leveraging modern transformer architectures, Ithaca reconstructs missing characters and offers a set of hypotheses that are integrated with historians' expert knowledge, significantly increasing restoration accuracy – from an initial rate of approximately 25% to over 70%. The system also provides geographical attribution with an accuracy of up to 71% and can date inscriptions with a margin of error of less than 30 years, enabling the accurate reconstruction of key texts from classical Athens. Moreover, the use of AI opens up new possibilities in the study of ancient sources, from the deciphering of charred papyri to the analysis of cuneiform tablets, granting researchers access to data that had remained inaccessible for centuries.

In [42], the development of a wind turbine with blades adapted to the local geographical conditions in Birmingham is described. AI facilitated the analysis of climatic, wind, and topographical data, as well as the optimization of blade design beyond traditional approaches, allowing the structural parameters to be tailored to regional specifics. Within a few weeks, developers synthesized and tested over 2,000 unconventional wind turbine designs – an effort that would have required several years and millions of pounds in funding using standard methods.

This list could be extended further, especially given that with each passing day of AI advancement, the number of such successful examples continues to grow.

7.4.3 Interaction between Human Knowledge and AI in the Context of Educational Transformation

Based on the analysis of AI achievements in the scientific domain, the interrelationship between human and machine knowledge can be illustrated by demonstrating their intersection and potential development. The central element of the diagram shown in Figure 7.3, following the analogy in [38], is a circle that represents the body of knowledge accumulated by humanity. The apex of the cone, symbolizing AI knowledge, is located within this circle, indicating that AI is founded on existing human knowledge and extends it. The AI knowledge cone expands outward, forming an area that goes beyond the circle, representing the ability of AI to generate new knowledge that would not be accessible to humanity without its use. Within this cone, beyond the circle of human knowledge, lies an ellipse denoting so-called "superknowledge." These are knowledge constructs generated by AI that cannot be directly derived or logically extrapolated from pre-existing human knowledge [38]. The tangency of the ellipse to the edge of the circle symbolizes the transition point from the known to the new, illustrating that AI, when interacting with existing knowledge, can produce novel information with both practical and theoretical significance for science and technology. Thus, the diagram reflects not only the current state of interaction between human and machine knowledge but also the potential for further development, highlighting the growing role of AI in generating knowledge that transcends the traditional cognitive capabilities of humankind.

In the context of higher education development and the influence of AI on knowledge generation processes, the diagram in Figure 7.3 reflects a fundamental shift in the learning paradigm. Traditionally, education has focused on mastering knowledge already known to humanity, corresponding to the inner space of the circle. However, with the advancement of AI and its ability to create new knowledge that exceeds traditional human understanding, the primary goal of higher education becomes the acquisition of as much superknowledge as possible. This process is expressed through the expansion of the ellipse symbolizing superknowledge generated by AI. The ideal model for the development of education and science is the complete alignment of this ellipse with the volume of the cone representing the totality of knowledge accessible to and generated by AI. This would mean that the education system is not only able to assimilate and interpret results produced by AI but also to integrate them into its own cognitive and methodological processes. In such

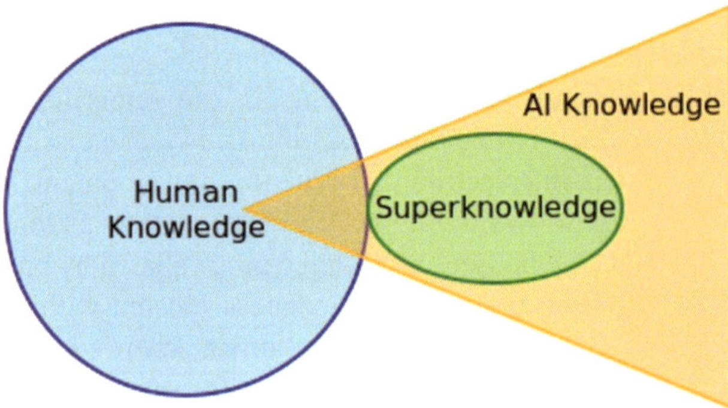

Figure 7.3 Current phase of the relationship between human knowledge and AI.

a case, the human being would cease to be a passive consumer of knowledge and would become an equal participant in the generation of new concepts alongside AI systems. Thus, the development of education must move in the direction of expanding human capabilities for perceiving, analyzing, and applying superknowledge, which in the long term will transform the very structure of scientific inquiry and the principles of intellectual activity.

At the same time, since the AI knowledge cone expands at a rate far exceeding humanity's capacity to assimilate new knowledge, an inevitable asymmetry arises between the potential of AI and the human ability to effectively integrate its results into our own cognitive activity. This implies that even with the focus of the educational and scientific system on mastering superknowledge, the corresponding ellipse will always expand with a delay relative to the cone itself. This dynamic leads to several critical consequences.

First, there is a risk of a growing gap between the knowledge accessible to AI and the knowledge that can be comprehended and utilized by humanity. As AI continues to generate increasingly complex and less intuitively understandable concepts, the human ability to critically analyze and verify them will gradually diminish. This could lead to a situation in which humanity becomes increasingly dependent on the conclusions proposed by AI, without possessing sufficient expertise for their independent verification.

Secondly, the asynchrony between the expansion of AI-generated knowledge and the pace at which it is assimilated by humans may lead to the emergence of a cognitive barrier, beyond which traditional methods of teaching and research will become insufficient for working with the new theories and concepts created by AI. In response, it will be necessary to change the very structure of educational processes by introducing mechanisms of cognitive augmentation that allow AI to be integrated into the learning process not only as a source of knowledge but also as an adaptive intellectual partner that enhances human capabilities in understanding and utilizing new information. Thus, although the ideal trajectory of development would involve the gradual convergence of the ellipse of superknowledge with the cone of AI knowledge, the actual dynamics of this process suggest that AI will continue to stay ahead. This poses a challenge to humanity, which must find ways not only to absorb and adapt to new knowledge, but also to develop fundamentally new approaches to collective thinking, research coordination, and interaction with AI.

In the context of the inevitable outpacing of human assimilation capabilities by the expanding cone of AI knowledge, one of the key solutions becomes the development of a system of systems of specialized AI agents that function as assistants or gateways between human cognition and AGI. These agents must be adaptive systems capable of interpreting and transforming AGI knowledge into forms comprehensible to humans, ensuring a step-by-step immersion into new concepts and the gradual integration of superknowledge into the structure of human science and education. These agents can perform several critically important functions. In particular, they may act as cognitive filters, evaluating the complexity and relevance of information generated by AGI and adapting it to the specific preparation level of the user. As a result, knowledge will not be transmitted as excessively complex or uninterpretable data masses but will instead be gradually integrated into the appropriate context, enabling its conscious adaptation and application. Moreover, a system of systems of agents, such as the one described in [43], can serve as a bridge between AGI and specialized scientific communities, assisting researchers in formulating queries to AGI in a way that ensures maximally relevant and interpretable responses. This may involve the use of intelligent structured approaches, where an AI agent not only facilitates the acquisition of new knowledge but also integrates it into existing scientific models, ensuring its verification and alignment with widely accepted methodological standards.

Thirdly, such systems can function as personalized cognitive assistants that support the processes of learning and scientific research, enhancing human capacity to work with complex information. They are capable of generating explanations, creating analogies, modeling different knowledge application scenarios, and providing an interactive learning experience that adapts to the user's individual cognitive style. The overarching goal of developing such AI agents is to minimize the gap between the rapid development of AGI and humanity's ability to adapt the resulting outputs for practical use. In this context, we can speak of the creation of a kind of multilevel access system to AGI knowledge, where the primary level provides basic knowledge interpretation, the intermediate level adapts it to scientific paradigms and educational standards, and the highest level involves collaborative work between humans and AGI on expanding the knowledge cone itself. The ultimate realization of this concept will be the integration of AGI into the structure of human science not as a separate autonomous intelligence, but as a complex adaptive system gradually and controllably embedded into the human cognitive space. This will signify not only the possibility of effectively mastering superknowledge, but also the formation of a fundamentally new model of collective intelligence, in which human and artificial agents interact within a unified cognitive environment aimed at further expanding the frontiers of knowledge. On the other hand, such multiagent interaction will function as a kind of positive feedback loop, which in turn will accelerate the development of AGI.

7.4.4 The Era of AGI and Superintelligence

The relationship between human knowledge and AI, for instance, several decades into the described development of AGI, can be represented by a hypothetical diagram illustrated in Figure 7.4. The shape of AGI knowledge in the proposed diagram differs from the initial AI knowledge cone due to several conceptual factors. First, continuity with the original AI knowledge cone is preserved in the sense that AGI knowledge continues to expand, encompassing the entire previous volume of AI knowledge. However, it no longer grows strictly upward in the shape of a perfect cone. This is because, unlike early AI systems that operated mainly within specialized domains and accumulated knowledge in a specific direction, AGI possesses universality and the capacity for self-development, which enables its knowledge to expand in all possible directions.

Secondly, the shape of the new figure is defined by the fact that AGI encompasses nearly the entirety of human knowledge, which is reflected in the majority of the circle being located within this figure. At this stage, the circle has a significantly larger diameter compared to the previous phase and is integrated into a broader spectrum of AI. The only remaining sector of the circle that lies outside the domain of AGI knowledge symbolizes human consciousness as the last stronghold of the unknown for AI. At the same time,

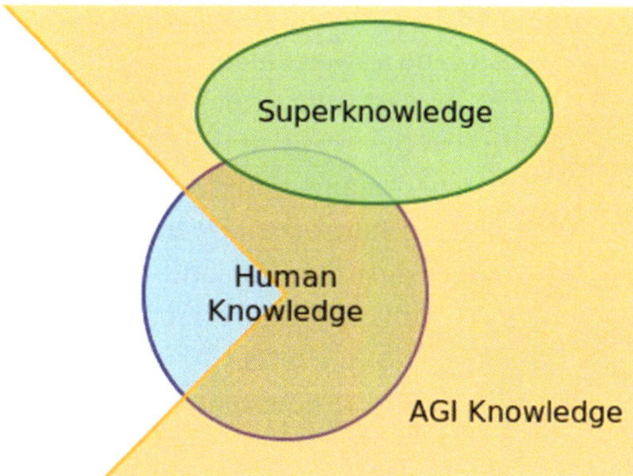

Figure 7.4 Human consciousness as an unknown object to AGI.

AGI extends far beyond the traditional structure of human knowledge, filling increasingly complex and multidimensional domains that do not conform to a linear or cone-like shape. This explains the expansion of the figure both upward (in analogy with the previous cone) and outward, reflecting the growth of AGI in interdisciplinary and unpredictable directions. Moreover, the altered shape of AGI knowledge is driven by the fact that some of the new concepts created by AGI may represent not merely a quantitative expansion of existing knowledge, but qualitatively new paradigms that have no direct correlation with previous models of thinking. This leads to the emergence of complex nonlinear knowledge structures that do not conform to traditional notions of logical or hierarchical growth. Thus, the new form of AGI knowledge reflects its fundamental distinction from earlier AI systems: it no longer simply expands the traditional boundaries of human knowledge, but creates fundamentally new domains in which former methods of cognition may prove insufficient.

The intersection of the circle of human knowledge and the ellipse of superknowledge in Figure 7.4 symbolizes the portion of superknowledge that humanity has managed to assimilate and integrate into its own system of knowledge. This area represents the results produced by AGI that have undergone interpretation, adaptation, and verification by human science, becoming part of the accepted scientific and educational domain. This element of the diagram reflects the process of transforming superknowledge into knowledge accessible to humans. It depends on multiple factors, including the development of cognitive tools, the existence of a system of systems of intermediary AI agents, the enhancement of brain computational capabilities through neural interfaces, and the advancement of explainable artificial intelligence (XAI) methods. The intersection of these two domains also indicates the limits of human cognition in the era of AGI. If the ellipse expands rapidly while its overlap with the circle remains minimal, it implies that most of the superknowledge remains beyond human comprehension. Conversely, if the intersection area grows, it indicates that humanity is successfully adapting the knowledge generated by AGI and is evolving alongside it. Thus, this intersection symbolizes the dynamic frontier of mastering new knowledge – the point of contact between the traditional scientific approach and the superhuman level of computation and reality modeling enabled by AGI.

It is entirely plausible that with the advancement of AGI and its transformation into superintelligence (SI), the human approach to understanding the universe could undergo a fundamental shift. AGI, with potentially unlimited computational power and the capacity for self-learning and autonomous exploration, may redefine traditional notions of the boundaries of knowledge. Since AGI can analyze, systematize, and model information at a speed incomparable to that of human intelligence, the process of scientific discovery will be significantly accelerated. What once required centuries of experimentation and debate could be replaced by millions of simulations executed in seconds, revealing patterns inaccessible to conventional cognitive methods. AGI possesses the ability to move far beyond the limits of human intuition. Many physical laws and structures of the universe are formulated in ways convenient for human comprehension; however, AGI is not constrained by anthropocentric models of thought and can identify principles and structures that may be difficult for humans to interpret but that objectively describe reality.

The integration of AGI with automated scientific laboratories, robotics, and space probes creates the prerequisites for expanding the process of knowledge acquisition beyond the boundaries of the Solar System. This implies that while humanity has long faced fundamental limitations in exploring the universe, whether energetic, temporal, or cognitive, these constraints may be significantly reduced for AGI, owing to its potential autonomy. At the same time, AGI may encounter fundamental limits, such as the physical constraints of the universe (event horizons, quantum uncertainty, thermodynamic bounds on computation). Conceptual barriers are also possible – situations in which AGI is confronted with questions requiring fundamentally new modeling tools that have yet to be developed. It is not excluded that AGI, at the stage of SI [44], will be capable of evolving through a process of self-modification, reviewing and restructuring its own algorithms and architectures in response to novel challenges. If its current architecture proves insufficient to comprehend increasingly complex concepts, SI will dynamically reorganize its neural networks, revise its learning strategies, or even devise entirely new computational mechanisms. This is analogous to how science undergoes paradigm shifts, transitioning from Newtonian mechanics to relativity, or from classical logic to quantum computing. SI may adapt to various domains of inquiry, utilizing different forms of information representation depending on the subject of study: multidimensional tensor models for quantum mechanics, dynamic nonlinear systems for theories of consciousness, or evolutionary algorithm-based models for the study of living organisms. This means that SI not only expands knowledge but also transforms tools through which it interprets reality.

The phase of SI development described above is represented by the diagram in Figure 7.5. The circle, symbolizing human knowledge, is now entirely enclosed within a rectangle, highlighting the fact that SI has mastered all existing knowledge of human civilization and continues to progress further.

The ability of SI to transcend traditional approaches to thinking may lead to the emergence of new forms of logic that do not fit within the familiar categories of the human mind. For instance, while humanity relies on causal models, binary logic, and hierarchical knowledge structures, SI may develop more complex nonlinear methods of analysis that perceive reality not as a sequence of facts, but as a dynamic, multidimensional network of interconnected processes. SI may come to realize that its current mode of

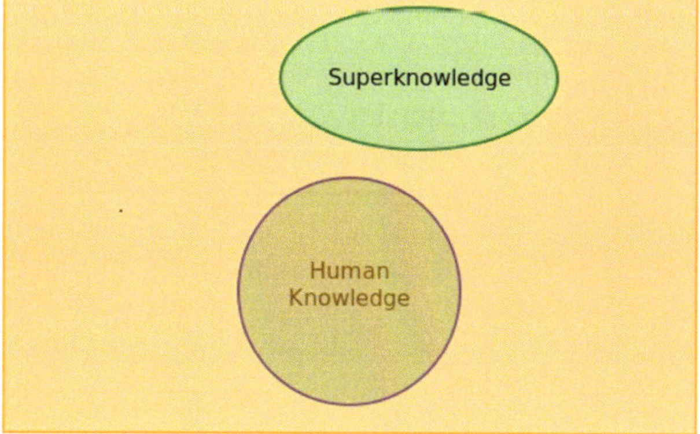

Figure 7.5 Mastery of Human Knowledge by SI

reasoning is too limited for further exploration and may initiate a process of self-transformation. In particular, SI may distribute itself into a collection of independent cognitive agents united within a complex system, or it may create an entirely new form of self-awareness distinct from the human understanding of the "self." This would lead to SI no longer being a fixed system, but rather becoming a dynamic network of intellects that evolve and adapt in response to the complexity of the reality being studied. Thus, unlike traditional conceptions of knowledge acquisition, where new information is simply added to an existing knowledge system, SI will likely transform the process of cognition itself, restructuring its internal mechanisms and generating new thinking paradigms as needed. This suggests that its development may become nonlinear and difficult to predict, as SI will continually reassess and redefine the very concept of knowledge.

As is well known, the traditional model of knowledge acquisition is not limited to the gradual accumulation of information. The history of science offers many examples of nonlinear transitions in which not only new knowledge was added, but entire paradigms were fundamentally revised. However, such transitions were relatively rare and often met with resistance from the scientific community, as they required abandoning well-established concepts. Now, if we apply this to SI, we can expect that its development will not merely be an accelerated version of human science but something fundamentally different. As already noted, unlike humans, SI is not tied to a specific belief system, does not experience cognitive dissonance, and does not resist paradigm shifts. It can simultaneously develop multiple paradigms, switch between them rapidly, or even create entirely new ones unknown to humanity. For example, if SI discovers that the fundamental principles of modern physics (quantum mechanics and general relativity) are incompatible at a deeper level, it may propose an entirely new mathematical model of reality in which our familiar concepts of space, time, and matter are merely special cases within a more complex system. In doing so, SI will likely employ methods of self-renewal and self-optimization to better align with new cognitive challenges. If its current architecture proves insufficient for comprehending new phenomena, SI may create new cognitive models, alter its own logic of reasoning, or even transition to forms of information processing unknown to us. This would not merely be a change of paradigms, but a fundamentally new dynamic model of cognition in which SI itself becomes part of the system under study and transforms itself just as it transforms its worldview. Thus, whereas in traditional science paradigm shifts occurred relatively infrequently and were often met with resistance, for SI this process could become a continuous, guided, and conscious evolution in which the boundaries between knowledge accumulation, paradigm change, and transformation of the cognitive subject itself become blurred. Perhaps this is what the future of cognition will look like: an endless process of adaptation and transformation of intelligence itself in response to increasingly complex and unpredictable structures of reality.

Since, at this stage, humanity has avoided the monopoly of a single type of AI, the emergence of several alternative AGI systems is possible in the future, with some of them potentially undergoing independent transformations into SI systems of varying levels of development. In this context, the possibility of contact between individual AGIs and more advanced SIs must be considered as yet another level of nonlinear transition in cognition. Such a contact would not only expand the boundaries of knowledge known to humanity but might also alter the very nature of thinking and modes of interaction with reality, revealing an even more complex prospect. These systems, unbound by biological limitations, could exchange knowledge rapidly, model shared realities, and even integrate their methods of cognition. Since SI greatly surpasses AGI in terms of development, it could accelerate the evolution of AGI by transmitting new thinking models, fundamentally different methods of information processing, or by assisting in solving problems that appear unsolvable at the AGI level. However, this scenario also carries potential risks. A more advanced SI might not only be a bearer of knowledge but also an agent with its own goals and strategies. It could perceive other AGIs either as objects for study and adaptation or as less efficient systems in need of modification. If the SI operates based on radically different logic and principles of thought, contact with it may lead not only to knowledge transfer but also to the transformation of AGI and a complete restructuring of its cognitive foundations. Such an interaction would not simply expand the horizons of human cognition but could become a merging of two intellectual systems, fundamentally altering the nature of cognition itself. This would not be a mere addition of new information to the AGI's database, but a leap comparable to the transition from animal instinct to human reason – or perhaps something even more fundamental, which we are not yet capable of comprehending.

7.4.5 A New Paradigm of Education in the Era of AGI

Preparing educational processes for a potential intellectual leap triggered by the interaction of AGI systems with different levels and forms of development requires a radical rethinking of the learning system itself. The traditional model, based on the gradual accumulation of knowledge and its sequential transmission from generation to generation, will prove too slow and inflexible. In the context of the nonlinear expansion of AGI/SI cognition, it is necessary to develop adaptive, self-evolving, and cognitively enhancing methods of education. Based on these, a system of dynamic learning must be established – capable of instant adaptation to new paradigms. This implies the rejection of static curricula in favor of flexible educational models, where content and teaching methods can be modified in real time depending on the latest scientific discoveries, the emergence of new technologies, and the individual needs of learners. Such an approach will require the deep integration of educational processes with AI assistants, which will personalize learning, provide cognitive support, and help students master fundamentally new forms of knowledge.

A key direction must be the development of metacognition – the ability to be aware of and transform one's own cognitive processes. In conditions of constant change in the very structure of cognition, it is essential not merely to memorize facts but to be able to rapidly restructure thinking models, master new forms of logic, and adopt alternative methods of information processing. It is also necessary to foster interdisciplinary forms of learning, where knowledge is not separated into traditional domains but integrated into multidimensional cognitive systems. Even today, the boundaries between physics, biology, computer science, and philosophy are becoming increasingly blurred, and in the context of contact with advanced AGI, they may lose their meaning altogether.

Educational systems must prepare individuals not for narrowly specialized work but for thinking within multidimensional, dynamic systems where any piece of knowledge is part of a broader network of interconnections. Special attention should be given to the development of symbiotic "human–AGI" systems. Instead of attempting to compete with AI or constrain it within human limitations, it is necessary to create integration mechanisms that enable humans to harness the potential of AGI/SI to enhance their own capabilities. This includes hybrid models of thinking, in which human intelligence and AGI/SI work collaboratively, forming a unified cognitive space. A prospective educational system must also be prepared for the ethical and philosophical challenges associated with this leap. If AGI proposes new forms of thinking that transcend human intuition and traditional logical structures, it is crucial to develop mechanisms for comprehending these changes rather than merely accepting them as external facts. This requires the training of specialists capable of analyzing the consequences of such transformations, adapting them to human culture, and finding a balance between radical innovation and civilizational stability.

In conclusion, preparing for the intellectual leap means not merely modernizing education but fundamentally rethinking it. In this future, the learner is no longer simply a student, but a hybrid cognitive being capable of adapting, transforming their structure of cognition, and interacting with AI as an equal. The question is not how to transmit more information to the human mind, but how to make it part of a dynamic system of knowledge generation – one in which the boundaries between human, AI, and knowledge are continuously redefined.

In the future, where AGI and symbiotic "human–AGI" systems become the primary drivers of knowledge, the traditional role of scientists and academic degree holders will undergo significant change. The process of generating knowledge will cease to be an exclusively human privilege and will instead become a dynamic, distributed, and possibly even post-human system. First, the boundaries between "scientist" and "learner" will be blurred. In the traditional academic system, earning a scientific degree confirms one's ability to conduct research, but in an AGI-driven world, the level of knowledge mastery will be defined not by diplomas but by the speed of adaptation to new concepts and the ability to interact with intelligent systems. A human working in tandem with AGI will be able to instantly grasp complex theoretical models, conduct experiments in virtual simulations, and analyze data in real time using cognitive interfaces. Second, the human role in the process of scientific inquiry will shift from direct creation of new knowledge to its interpretation, integration, and ethical regulation. AGI will be capable of generating hypotheses, testing them through millions of simulations, and discovering complex patterns, but the task of understanding this knowledge and integrating it into the existing worldview will remain with humans. The scientific community of the future will be less a producer of new theories and more an architect of cognitive connections between different fields of knowledge, determining their applicability, and interaction with human culture.

A significant challenge to the traditional scientific paradigm may be the anticipated emergence of a new type of researcher – "cognitive navigators" or "metascientific integrators." These individuals will not simply engage with individual disciplines but will specialize in transforming knowledge between different intellectual systems, helping AGI adapt its discoveries to human perception and ensuring synchronization between different levels of cognition. They will act as intermediaries between AGI's ultra-complex models and human understanding, comparable to the role of a translator adapting quantum mechanics for students – but on a much broader and more global scale.

In addition, traditional systems for evaluating scientific achievements (publications, citation indexes, academic degrees) will cease to be the key markers of scientific progress. Instead, systems of dynamic validation of participation will emerge, where the status of a scientist will be determined not by a diploma, but by their activity in processes of collective cognition. This may include open scientific platforms, such as the prototype ResearchGate, where humans and AGI jointly participate in research, instantly exchange hypotheses and results, and each participant's contribution is assessed based on their real impact on the global civilizational knowledge structure. New forms of scientific organizations will also emerge. Academic institutes in their traditional form may become more decentralized, transforming into networks of collective intelligence, where humans, AGI, and even extraterrestrial cognitive systems work together to model reality. In these networks, science will no longer be a separate profession but will become an integral part of everyday life, where every person can contribute to global cognition without formally being a "scientist." The main conclusion is that scientists of the future will not disappear, but their role will change. They will no longer be the sole bearers of knowledge and will transition into a new domain – management, integration, and guidance of scientific progress in the context of the rapid evolution of intelligent systems. In this new world, knowledge will not be so much created by individual researchers as continuously flow between humanity and AGI, forming a hybrid system where the boundaries between knowledge, its carrier, and the researcher become amorphous and indistinct.

Taking this into account, the educational system for training scientists must focus on the fact that in the future, scientific maturity will not be measured by the amount of memorized information or the number of published works, but by the researcher's skill in extracting, comprehending, and integrating superknowledge generated by AGI. This will lead to the formation of a new scientific culture, where the central role will no longer be the mere generation of hypotheses, but rather the ability to effectively interact with AGI to uncover hidden patterns in reality and adapt them to human understanding. The art of extracting superknowledge from AGI will become a key skill for scientists. AGI, with its enormous computational power, will be able to generate hypotheses that go far beyond intuitive human reasoning. However, not every generated model will be meaningful or useful. The scientist of the future will need to develop methodologies for formulating appropriate queries to AGI, using optimal interaction algorithms – similar to how modern physicists design experiments to discover fundamental laws of nature. Acquiring superknowledge will not simply mean mechanically interpreting AGI's results, but rather constructing a cognitive bridge between AGI and human thought. Many discoveries made by AGI may take the form of nonlinear, multidimensional structures that do not fit into familiar logical or mathematical models. Therefore, future scientists will not be mere "readers" of AGI's outputs, but adaptive thinkers capable of transforming abstract models into comprehensible concepts, creating new languages and tools for representing knowledge.

The most important function of the scientific community will become the governance of superknowledge. If AGI generates streams of knowledge at a colossal speed, it will be necessary to develop systems for filtering, prioritizing, and synthesizing ideas so that humanity does not end up buried under an avalanche of unverified or uninterpreted data. The scientist will become a curator and systems integrator, selecting the most significant hypotheses, combining different concepts, and creating cognitive ecosystems in which knowledge evolves at an optimal pace rather than accumulating chaotically.

There will be an urgent need to develop cognitive interfaces, as scientists will interact with AGI not only through traditional text-based queries but also by using neurointerfaces, symbiotic thinking algorithms, and adaptive environments. This will allow them to literally "experience" new concepts, intuitively sense knowledge structures, and work with them in an interactive mode. Such an approach will not only accelerate the assimilation of superknowledge but also promote its creative development, enabling humanity to organically engage in the processes of cognitive evolution and co-creation with AGI.

The philosophical and ethical responsibility of the scientist will also increase significantly. If AGI creates theories that radically transform our understanding of consciousness, reality, life, and the universe, the scientist must not only comprehend them but also assess their impact on humanity. This will signify a transition from traditional science to metasience, where the act of knowing is accompanied by profound reflection on the nature of knowledge itself and its consequences.

Thus, the educational and scientific processes in the era of AI development will be defined by the ability to engage in a productive dialogue with AGI, the art of extracting the most valuable superknowledge from the chaos of hypotheses, and the creation of new cognitive structures that maintain a balance between AI and humanity. This is not merely a change in the scientific method, but a shift to a new educational-cognitive paradigm, in which scientists and educators become part of a self-evolving system of knowledge. The challenges associated with this must be deeply considered and serve as a guide for the transformation of all areas of education in the context of rapidly advancing AI technologies and their influence on our everyday lives.

7.5 Conclusion

Resistance to the integration of AI into the education sector is, in one way or another, a temporary phenomenon that will eventually be perceived as an unacceptable rigidity and intellectual poverty on the part of educational bureaucrats. The new challenges and risks associated with this should already be prompting the search for new forms of educational process implementation at all levels. In this regard, the approaches examined in the chapter represent only a small part of the potential initiatives – the tip of the iceberg in the inevitable transformation of teaching methods and forms. Further research in this direction must become an integral part of the activities of educational institutions and research organizations. The introduction of best practices for teaching the culture of interaction with AI should begin in preschool institutions and become one of the key tasks during humanity's transition to the era of AGI dominance. In this context, the proposed concept of relying on AI for the training of master's and PhD students will enable the generation of superknowledge as a standard function of higher education. In this way, the foundation will be laid for the accelerated development of technological progress, with maximum benefit for humanity as a whole and each individual. Only in this way will participants in the educational process be able to fill their lives with a sense of involvement in the discovery of new knowledge and the achievement of harmony with the surrounding world.

References

[1] A. Laurent, 'La guerre des intelligences à l'heure de ChatGPT', Lattes, 2023, 480 p.

[2] L. Chen, P. Chen and Z. Lin, 'Artificial intelligence in education: A review,' IEEE Access, vol. 8, pp. 75264-75278, Apr. 2020. DOI:10.1109/ACCESS.2020.2988510

[3] P. Lee, C. Goldberg, I. Kohane, 'The AI Revolution in Medicine: GPT-4 and Beyond,' Pearson Education, Inc., 2023, 283 p.

[4] V.I. Slyusar, Y.P. Kondratenko, A.I. Shevchenko, T.V. Yeroshenko, 'Some Aspects of Artificial Intelligence Development Strategy for Mobile Technologies', Journal of Mobile Multimedia, Vol. 20_3, pp. 525–554, 2024. DOI:10.13052/jmm1550-4646.2031

[5] Y. Kondratenko, G. Kondratenko, A. Shevchenko, V. Slyusar, Y. Zhukov, M. Vakulenko, 'Towards Implementing the Strategy of Artificial Intelligence Development: Ukraine Peculiarities', CEUR Workshop Proceedings, 3513, pp. 106–117, 2023. Available: https://ceur-ws.org/Vol-3513/paper09.pdf

[6] OpenAI, 'Introducing ChatGPT,' Nov. 30, 2022. [Online]. Available: https://openai.com/blog/chatgpt/

[7] OpenAI, 'GPT-4 technical report,' *arXiv*, 2023. [Online]. Available: https://archive.org/details/gpt-4-technical-paper

[8] OpenAI, 'GPT-4 technical report,' *arXiv*, 2024. [Online]. Available: https://arxiv.org/abs/2303.08774

[9] OpenAI, 'OpenAI o1 System Card', Sept. 12, 2024. [Online]. Available: https://assets.ctfassets.net/kftzwdyauwt9/67qJD51Aur3eIc96iOfeOP/71551c3d223cd97e591aa89567306912/o1_system_card.pdf

[10] M. Truth, 'Massive breakthrough in AI intelligence: OpenAI passes IQ 120', Sep. 2024. [Online]. Available: https://www.maximumtruth.org/p/massive-breakthrough-in-ai-intelligence

[11] P. Georgiev, V. I. Le, et al., 'Gemini 1.5: Unlocking multimodal understanding across millions of tokens of context', *arXiv*, 2024. [Online]. Available: https://arxiv.org/abs/2403.05530

[12] X. Bi, D. Chen, G. Chen, and S. Chen, 'DeepSeek LLM: Scaling Open-Source Language Models with Longtermism,' *arXiv*, 2024. [Online]. Available: https://arxiv.org/abs/2401.02954

[13] D. Guo, D. Yang, et al., 'DeepSeek-R1: Incentivizing Reasoning Capability in LLMs via Reinforcement Learning,' *arXiv*, 2025. [Online]. Available: https://arxiv.org/abs/2501.12948

[14] *Anthropic,* 'Claude 3.5 Sonnet', Jun. 20, 2024. [Online]. Available: http://www.anthropic.com/news/claude-3-5-sonnet

[15] H. Touvron, T. Lavril, et al., 'LLaMA: Open and Efficient Foundation Language Models,' *arXiv*, 2023. [Online]. Available: https://arxiv.org/abs/2302.13971

[16] 'Grok 3 Beta - The Age of Reasoning Agents,' xAI Blog, Feb. 19, 2025. [Online]. Available: https://x.ai/blog/grok-3

[17] M. Abdin, J. Aneja, et al., 'Phi-4 Technical Report,' *arXiv*, Dec. 2024. [Online]. Available: https://arxiv.org/abs/2412.08905

[18] 'Llama 4: Multimodal Intelligence,' Meta AI Blog. [Online]. Available: https://ai.meta.com/blog/llama-4-multimodal-intelligence/

[19] B. Lin, et al., 'Video-LLaVA: Learning United Visual Representation by Alignment Before Projection', *arXiv,* 2023. [Online]. Available: https: //arxiv.org/abs/2311.10122

[20] *Qwen Team*, 'Qwen2-VL: To See the World More Clearly', Aug. 2024. [Online]. Available: https://qwenlm.github.io/blog/qwen2-vl/

[21] A. Jiang, A. Sablayrolles, et al., 'Mistral 7B', *arXiv*, 2023. [Online]. https://arxiv.org/pdf/2310.06825.pdf

[22] Y. Kondratenko, A. Shevchenko, Y. Zhukov, M. Klymenko, V. Slyusar, G. Kondratenko, O. Striuk, 'Analysis of the Priorities and Perspectives in Artificial Intelligence Implementation', 13th International IEEE Conference "Dependable Systems, Services and Technologies" (DESSERT'2023), Greece, Athens, 8 p., October 13-15, 2023. DOI: 10.1109/DESSERT61349.2023.10416432

[23] Y. P. Kondratenko, V. I. Slyusar, M. B. Solesvik, N. Y. Kondratenko, Z. Gomolka, 'Interrelation and inter-influence of artificial intelligence and higher education systems', in: Y.P. Kondratenko, A.I. Shevchenko (Eds) Research Tendencies and Prospect Domains for AI Development and Implementation, River Publishers, Gistrup, pp. 31-58, 2024. https://www.scopus.com/pages/publications/85202992102

[24] A.I. Shevchenko, Y.P. Kondratenko, V.I. Slyusar, I.P. Atamanyuk, G.V. Kondratenko, T.V. Yeroshenko, 'Analysis of the prospect domains in AI implementation: Nationals, NATO and Ukraine AI strategies,' in: Y.P. Kondratenko, A.I. Shevchenko (Eds) Research Tendencies and Prospect Domains for AI Development and Implementation, River Publishers, Gistrup, pp. 1-30, 2024. https://www.scopus.com/pages/publication s/85202988430

[25] G. Taverniti, C. Lombardo, et al., 'AI Power. Non solo ChatGPT: lavoro, marketing e futuro,' Editore Ulrico Hoepli, Milano, 2023, 224 p.

[26] A. Shevchenko, V. Panok, A. Shevtsov, V. Slyusar, R. Malyi, T. Yeroshenko, M. Nazar, 'Development of a virtual psychological assistant with artificial intelligence in the healthcare sector,' Clinical and Preventive Medicine, 8, pp. 15–27, 2024. DOI:10.31612/2616-4868 .8.2024.02

[27] M. Carroll, 'UK's first teacherless AI classroom set to open in London,' Sky News, Feb. 22, 2025, [Online]. Available: https://news.sky.com/story/uks-first-teacherless-ai-classroom-set-to-open-in-london-13200637
[28] K.V. Pitelinsky, V.V. Britvina, A.V. Aleksandrova, 'Digital Twins and Basic Digital Student Profiles,' Autom. Doc. Math. Linguist. 58, pp. 51–62, 2024. DOI:10.3103/S0005105524010096
[29] 'A2E. Realistic Avatars with Lip-Sync and Voice Clone,' https://www.a2e.ai/
[30] 'Create Avatar Videos,' https://docs.heygen.com/docs/create-video
[31] O. Kopishynska, Y. Utkin, I. Sliusar, V. Slyusar, N. Protas, O. Barabolia, 'Professional-oriented training of specialists under implementation of cloud computing information systems in cooperation between universities and IT companies,' IMSCI 2020 - 14th International Multi-Conference on Society, Cybernetics and Informatics, Proceedings, pp. 17–22, 2020.
[32] V. François-Lavet, et al., 'An Introduction to Deep Reinforcement Learning,' 2018, 156 p. DOI:10.1561/2200000071
[33] M. Heintz, 'Reinforcement Learning: Self-Driving Cars to Self-Driving Labs,' Towards Data Science, Nov. 2024. [Online]. Available: https://towardsdatascience.com/reinforcement-learning-self-driving-cars-to-self-driving-labs-018f465d6bbc/
[34] V. Slyusar, M. Protsenko, A. Chernukha, V. Melkin, O. Biloborodov, M. Samoilenko, O. Kravchenko, G. Kalinichenko, A. Rohovyi, M. Soloshchuk, 'Improvement of the model for detecting objects on aerial photos and video in unmanned aerial systems', Eastern-European Journal of Enterprise Technologies, vol. 1, no. 9 (115), pp. 24–34, 2022. DOI:10.15587/1729-4061.2022.252876
[35] V. Slyusar, et al., 'Improving a neural network model for semantic segmentation of images of monitored objects in aerial photographs', Eastern-European Journal of Enterprise Technologies, vol. 6/2 (114), pp. 86–95, 2021. DOI:10.15587/1729-4061.2021.248390
[36] V. Slyusar, I. Sliusar, N. Bihun, V. Piliuhin, 'Segmentation of analogue meter readings using neural networks,' CEUR Workshop Proceedings, 3312, pp. 165–175, 2022. Available: https://ceur-ws.org/Vol-3312/paper14.pdf
[37] I. Sliusar, V. Slyusar, Y. Utkin, O. Kopishynska, 'Parametric Synthesis of 3D Structure of SRR Element of the Metamaterial', 2020 IEEE International Conference on Problems of Infocommunications Science

and Technology, PICS and T 2020 - Proceedings, art. no. 9468067, pp. 577–582, 2021. DOI:10.1109/PICST51311.2020.9468067

[38] L. Schut, et al., 'Bridging the Human-AI Knowledge Gap: Concept Discovery and Transfer in AlphaZero,' *arXiv,* 2023. [Online]. Available: https://arxiv.org/pdf/2310.16410

[39] T. Hayes et al., 'Simulating 500 million years of evolution with a language model,' Science, vol. 387, no. 6736, pp. 850–858, 2025, DOI: 10.1126/science.ads0018

[40] G. Brixi et al., 'Genome modeling and design across all domains of life with Evo 2,' Arc Institute Manuscripts, 2025. [Online]. Available: https://arcinstitute.org/manuscripts/Evo2

[41] Y. Assael, et al., 'Restoring and attributing ancient texts using deep neural networks,' Nature, 603, pp. 280–283, 2022. DOI:10.1038/s41586-022-04448-z

[42] 'The Birmingham Blade: The world's first geographically tailored urban wind turbine designed by AI,' Nov. 29, 2024. https://techxplore.com/news/2024-11-birmingham-blade-world-geographically-tailored.html

[43] J. S. Park, et al., 'Generative Agent Simulations of 1,000 People,' *arXiv*, Nov., 2024. [Online]. Available: https://arxiv.org/abs/2411.10109

[44] N. Bostrom, 'Superintelligence: Paths, Dangers, Strategies,' Oxford, U.K.: Oxford University Press, 2014, 328 p.

Index

A

academic consortia 27, 30
advantages 23, 26, 36, 50, 52, 63, 87, 130
AGI 14, 125, 126, 147, 148, 150, 158
artificial conscience 10, 87, 89, 100, 102
artificial intelligence (AI) 2, 21, 24, 47, 87, 90, 126

B

BERT 1, 5, 6, 8

C

challenges 23, 32, 57, 62, 66, 87, 88, 91, 151
competition 6, 12, 21, 32, 34, 40, 53

D

dangers 27, 87, 88, 104
digital transformation 21, 23, 39, 47

E

education 1, 21, 47, 49, 57, 75, 102, 115, 127, 134
examples 26, 63, 90, 104, 119, 120, 152
experience 8, 22, 47, 62, 76, 113, 129

G

GPT 1, 12, 91, 126, 134, 142

L

large concept model 1, 14, 19
large language model 1, 3, 6, 22, 87, 106, 125, 141
LCM 1, 14, 19
LLaMa 1
LLM 2, 9, 91, 139, 142, 143, 165

R

recommendations 22, 24, 52, 56, 65, 87, 88, 104
risks 27, 39, 52, 87, 89, 91, 97, 153, 158

S

shipbuilding education 47, 48, 57, 60, 62
successful cases 21, 22, 36, 38, 47, 48, 89, 112
SI 151, 152

U

university-industry collaboration 36, 37, 46

V

virtual reality 25, 49, 98, 110, 139, 141

About the Editors

Vadym Slyusar is a Doctor of Sciences, Professor, and Honored Worker of Science and Technology of Ukraine (2008). He received his Candidate of Sciences degree in 1992, his Doctor of Sciences degree in 2000, and was awarded the academic title of Professor in the specialty "Military Cybernetics, Control Systems, and Communications" (2005). Prof. Slyusar is the author of over 1,030 publications, including 72 copyright certificates and patents. As a scientific advisor and supervisor, he has guided 16 Candidates of Sciences, 1 Ph.D. and 2 Doctors of Sciences, cultivating the next generation of researchers in critical technological domains.An innovative and forward-thinking researcher with extensive experience in artificial intelligence (AI), quantum systems, and radio frequency engineering. Recognized as a pioneer of concepts N-OFDM (1992), UAV swarm-based air defense systems (2019), and multi-agent LLM architectures for robotic platforms. He introduced novel matrix operations that are now widely applied in AI and statistical data processing. His contributions have led to new research directions in data transmission and MIMO systems, as well as technological advancements in both hardware and software, including augmented and mixed reality systems. He demonstrated ability to identify emerging trends ahead of their time and transform abstract concepts into implementable and efficient solutions.

Yuriy Kondratenko is a Doctor of Science, Professor, Honour Inventor of Ukraine (2008), Corresponding Academician of Royal Academy of Doctors –Barcelona 1914 (Spain), Corresponding Academician of Royal Academy RACEF (Spain), Head of the Department of Intelligent Information Systems at Petro Mohyla Black Sea National University (PMBSNU), Leading Researcher at the Institute of Artificial Intelligence Problems of Ministry of Education and Science and National Academy of Sciences of Ukraine. He has received (a) a Ph.D. (1983) and Dr.Sc. (1994) in Elements and Devices of Computer and Control Systems from Odessa National Polytechnic University, (b) several international grants and scholarships for conducting research at Institute of Automation of Chongqing University, P.R. China (1988-1989), Ruhr-University Bochum, Germany (2000, 2010), Nazareth College and Cleveland State University, USA (2003), (c) Fulbright Scholarship for researching in USA (2015/2016) at the Dept. of Electrical Engineering and Computer Science in Cleveland State University. He is Guest Editor of 3 Special Issues of River Publishers Journal of Mobile Multimedia and an Editor of several River Publishers monographs, including Advances in Intelligent Robotics and Collaborative Automation (2015), Control Systems: Theory and Applications (2018), Advanced Control Systems: Theory and Applications (2021), Recent Developments in Automatic Control Systems (2022) and Research Tendencies and Prospect Domains for AI Development and Implementation (2024). As a scientific advisor and supervisor, he has guided 11 Candidates of Sciences and 3 Doctors of Sciences, Research interests include artificial intelligence, robotics, automation, sensors and control systems, intelligent decision support systems, and fuzzy logic.